# The Occasional Papers

## OF THE

# Standing Liturgical Commission

**Collection Number One**

The Church Hymnal Corporation
800 Second Avenue, New York, NY 10017

# Contents

Introduction   **v**

The Three-Year Eucharistic Lectionary   **1**
    *Reginald H. Fuller*

The Passion of Witness: Prolegomena
to the Revision of the Sanctoral Calendar   **12**
    *Thomas J. Talley*

The Liturgy in Easter Season   **18**
    *Michael W. Merriman*

Rites of Initiation   **24**
    *Charles P. Price*

The Power and the Promise of Language in
Worship: Inclusive Language Guidelines for the Church   **38**
    *Robert A. Bennett*

The Musical Implications
of The Book of Common Prayer   **51**
    *Louis Weil*

Architectural Implications
of The Book of Common Prayer   **57**
    *Marion J. Hatchett*

The Proposed Lesser Feasts & Fasts
as Approved for Trial Use, 1985–1988   **68**

# Introduction

A series of Occasional Papers on liturgical subjects was inaugurated by the Standing Commission during the 1982–1985 Triennium, with the authorization of the General Convention. Originally distributed individually in typescript form to diocesan Bishops and diocesan liturgical committees, with permission to reproduce them locally, reprints have been supplied upon request. The supply of such reprints has been exhausted. In order to make the Papers more accessible, the seven numbers already issued have been here collected and published by The Church Hymnal Corporation, which also plans to publish future collections of Papers from time to time. Individual Papers will also be issued by the Liturgical Commission as they are produced, and will be distributed, as were the original numbers, to the same diocesan recipients.

Although all of the Occasional Papers have been approved by the Standing Liturgical Commission, each has been written by a selected author and manifests that author's distinctive style. No attempt has been made to conform to a single style throughout the collection.

This Hymnal Corporation publication also includes the Propers and biographical notes for the additional commemorations in the Church Year Calendar which were proposed by the General Convention of 1985 for trial use. If they are approved by the forthcoming Convention, they will be included in a subsequent edition of *Lesser Feasts and Fasts.*

The Rev. Canon Charles Mortimer Guilbert,
*Custodian of the Standard Book of Common Prayer*
*March, 1987*

# The Three-Year Eucharistic Lectionary

## The Reverend Reginald H. Fuller

*November 1982*

The three-year eucharistic lectionary is widely acclaimed to be the most accepted part of the new Book of Common Prayer. During the trial period, it met with next to no opposition, and everyone perceived its value. We Episcopalians owe an incalculable debt to the Reverend Dr. Massey Shepherd for its introduction into our Prayer Book. Dr. Shepherd was a member of the International Commission on English Texts (ICET) and an influential member of the Standing Liturgical Commission just at the time when our own liturgical revision was beginning. He therefore knew what hardly anyone else knew, outside of Roman Catholic circles; that the Roman Catholic Church had begun to construct a three-year eucharistic lectionary. He saw to it that this lectionary became part of the new Prayer Book and was adapted for the Episcopal Church.

## The Gospels

The lectionary of the 1928 Prayer Book was, with slight revisions, essentially that of Sarum, which, in turn, was a North European variant of the medieval Roman lectionary. It was therefore

1

natural that when Rome revised, we should do so, too. A revision was long overdue. The old Epistles and Gospels provided but a meager selection of Holy Scripture. Overwhelmingly, the Gospels were from St. Matthew. Luke came way behind, and Mark occurred only two or three times a year (and all of those occasions, except one, were introduced by the revision of the Prayer Book in 1928). Today, most modern scholars value Mark more highly than our forebears did because they believe that Mark was the earliest gospel, and is therefore in closest touch with the Jesus of history.

The second reason for change is that in recent years far more attention is being paid to the Evangelists as theologians in their own right—the movement known as redaction criticism. That is why each Evangelist is now given a year of his own, so that we have a Matthew Year (A); a Year of Mark (B), supplemented by John, because Mark is the shortest gospel (see Propers 13 16B); and a Luke Year (C). Otherwise, John is use during the Christmas season, in the period from Ash Wednesday to Pentecost and on certain fixed festivals. The Lenten Gospels especially in Year A form a Johannine course of instruction in preparation for the Easter baptisms.

Each of the Gospels is read more or less in course—unlike the old Prayer Book Gospels, which appear chopped and changed all over the place. In this way, most of what was worth reading publicly in all four Gospels is covered. The Scriptures are now opened up to the people as never before. Thus, one of the major goals of the Reformers—now shared with Rome, has at last been attained.

## The Epistles

The Epistles pose a somewhat more difficult problem. Everyone is agreed that the traditional selection was far from ideal. The 1928 Prayer Book had some of the most difficult epistle readings in the New Testament. Older people will not forget old Lent IV with its mystifying allegory about Sarah and Hagar; or Trinity XIII, with Paul's argument about seed and seeds (Galatians 3:16). Such rabbinic exegesis was incomprehensible to the average churchgoer, and probably to the clergy, too. There were also some relics of an earlier continuous reading—e.g., Romans, 1 Corinthians, and Galatians in the post-Trinity season. Obviously, we had to go back and start again from scratch. The Sundays and festivals during the first part of the Church Year often had traditional readings which could re-

2

main undisturbed (e.g., Colossians 3:1–4 for Easter Day). But during the "green seasons" which the Romans usefully call "ordinary time," it was possible to work through the epistles, selecting in order the most suitable readings each one offered. Thus to take these seasons in Year A the Epistles covered are:

**Post-Epiphany**
    1 Corinthians (early chapters)

**Post-Pentecost**
    1 Corinthians (early chapters continued)
    Romans (Propers 4–19)
    Philippians (4 Sundays)
    1 Thessalonians (5 Sundays)

The selections in Years B and C are made on similar principles.

Clerics and Lay Readers often complain that they are hard put to it to find some continuous theme between the Epistles and the Gospels. The answer is, there isn't meant to be one. Occasionally, a common theme may be discernible to the ingenious homilist, but such connections are undesigned coincidences. The fact is, if one wants continuous reading for both Epistles and Gospels, one cannot have thematic correspondence. And, in any case, "theme preaching" is one of the major homiletical crimes, at least in German Lutheranism, where the present writer had part of his theological education.

Two further seasons merit comment, before we leave the Epistles. One is the Lenten season. The Epistles here tend to correspond to the Old Testament Readings. Thus, for instance, on Lent 1 in Year A, the reading from Romans 5:12–19 is about Christ as the Second Adam, corresponding to Genesis 1, the creation of the first Adam. Similarly, the Romans 4 Lesson about Abraham as the model of Christian faith corresponds to the call of Abraham (Genesis 12:1–8). The reason for this change in policy is that the Old Testament readings in Lent have a special character of their own (see below). The other Season that calls for comment is that of Easter. In Year A, the Epistle readings are from I Peter, which was, from the very earliest times, associated with Easter and Baptism. In Year B the Epistle readings are from I John, also full of baptismal allusions; while in Year C the second, or New Testament Reading (it ought not to be called "Epistle"—that is a hangover from the old Prayer Book), is from Revelation, another book which was traditionally read during this Season. This was because of its pictures of heavenly worship, rather than for its futurist eschatology, which comes more appropriately in late post-Pentecost and in early Advent.

## The Old Testament Readings

One of the major shortcomings of the old eucharistic readings was their almost total neglect of the Old Testament. In early days, there were three lessons, the first from the Old Testament or Apocrypha. This reading was dropped before the separation of East and West, except on a few occasions, when the Epistle or New Testament Reading was dropped instead (see the Sunday before Advent in the 1928 Prayer Book, where the Old Testament Lesson has survived, and there is no "Epistle"). The new lectionary has reverted to the ancient practice (except in the Easter season and on some Saints' days, when Acts is used instead of the Old Testament, see below).

The Old Testament readings are not chosen in course. Instead, except during Lent, they are selected to match the Gospel readings. This means that the Old Testament is treated christologically, either as prediction or as type. Predictive readings are especially characteristic of Advent—e.g., Advent 2 in Year B, where Isaiah 40:1–11 matches the ministry of John the Baptist (Mark 1:1–8). Typological interpretation means that an object, a person, or an institution in the Old Testament is regarded as foreshadowing in some way some aspect of the Christ event and its salvific consequences. An example of typological matching would be Proper 4 in Year C, where the Gospel is the raising of the widow's son at Nain (Luke 7:1–10), complemented by Elisha's raising of a widow's son in 1 Kings 8.

The Lenten Readings from the Old Testament do not match the Gospel reading, but in each year provide a conspectus of salvation history. For instance, in Year A we have:

Lent 1, The creation of Adam and Eve (Gen. 2)
Lent 2, The call of Abraham (Gen. 12)
Lent 3, The water from the Rock in the Wilderness (Exod. 17)
Lent 4, The anointing of David (1 Sam. 16:1–13)
Lent 5, Ezekiel's vision of the dry bones (Ezek. 37)

Years B and C each provide a different series of highlights of salvation history.

## Changes from the Roman Catholic Lectionary

As already mentioned, the Episcopal Church has made its own adaptation of the Roman Catholic lectionary. On what principles were these adaptations made? Some of the changes were occasioned by a difference of calendar. Basically, we have the same calendar, of course, as, indeed, our old calendar in the 1928 Prayer Book stemmed from the Sarum version of the North European calendar, which again was slightly different from the calendar used south of the Alps (hence, *e.g.*, the Sundays "after Trinity" instead of "after Pentecost"). One major dislocation between Rome and ourselves occurs at the beginning of Lent. By a curious historical accident Rome has traditionally read the account of the Transfiguration on Lent 2. For us, Lent 2 has never had this association. During the early stages of the revision, Dr. Shepherd came up with a brilliant suggestion (derived from Lutheran practice) of using the Transfiguration for the (invariable) last Sunday after Epiphany. That episode is at once the culmination of the epiphanies in the Galilean ministry, which the previous Sundays have celebrated, and also, especially in the Lucan form of the story used in Year C, the curtain-raiser to the journey up to Jerusalem and the Passion. Unfortunately, this results in a dislocation in Lent 2, where we have replaced the Roman Transfiguration gospel as follows:

Year A, John 3:1–17. The Nicodemus discourse
Year B, Mark 8:31–38. The cost of discipleship
Year C, Luke 13:31–35. Jesus' prediction of his Passion

Prior to the Draft Book of 1976, we had another major difference with Rome. A perennial problem with all lectionaries is the variable date of Easter and the consequent difference in each year of the number of Sundays after Epiphany and Pentecost (Trinity). The old Prayer Book solved this difficulty by providing 25 Sundays after Trinity and a rubric (p. 224) borrowing extra Sundays from the last two Sundays of the post-Epiphany season when required. Extra Sundays at the end of the post-Trinity season were dropped when not required. Rome had initially proposed to follow the same system in its new lectionary. But after we had adapted the new lectionary for the first trial book (the "Green Book"), Rome came up with

5

a new system of "Sundays of the Year," beginning after Epiphany, running through the last Sunday before Ash Wednesday, then picking up again after Pentecost and running to Advent. The extra Sundays were dropped *not* at the end of the post-Pentecost season, but between post-epiphany and post-Pentecost. It was too late for us to change in 1971, and so for five years we were often two or three Sundays out of step with Rome. Unfortunately, too, other Churches, which were making their own modifications of the Roman lectionary, such as the Lutherans, followed us rather than Rome. But then, as we were preparing the final revision for the draft book of 1976, Captain Howard Galley, C.A., Editorial Assistant to the Coordinator of Prayer Book Revision, came up with an excellent suggestion. He noted the old Prayer Book rule for the date of Advent Sunday: it was to fall on the Sunday nearest to St. Andrew's Day (November 30). This gave Capt. Galley the idea of working backwards, a week at a time. The last Sunday after Pentecost would have its fixed proper on the Sunday nearest to November 23, and so on, backwards to the Sunday closest to May 11, the earliest possible date for the Feast of Pentecost. Then the propers were numbered forward from that Sunday as Proper 1, Proper 2, and so on. One price that has to be paid for this ingenious system is that the Sundays after Pentecost have no fixed Propers of their own. But it is a price that is ecumenically worth paying. It also means that the readings of the last three Sundays after Pentecost are always eschatological, dealing with the final consummation. This theme runs through Advent 1, so that the years always overlap and thus are welded together. This, too, explains why, on the first Sunday of Advent, we start the new series of Gospel readings with eschatological material toward the end of the Gospel that is to be read in that year. Thus, Advent 1 in Year A has Matthew 24:37–44, and it is Advent 2, not Advent 1, that begins with Matthew 3:1–13.

The Roman Catholics, naturally, use more of the Apocrypha than we do, for these books are for them part of the canonical scripture, in a way that they are not for us (the Anglican attitude to the Apocrypha is stated in Article VI of the Articles of Religion, *BCP,* pp. 868–869). Consequently, we have reduced somewhat the number of apocryphal readings, though there are more in the new lectionary than there have ever been in Anglican use before. This, also, gave us an opportunity to feature more strongly the social teaching of the prophets. For instance, for Proper 27 in Year A, Amos

5:1–24 replaces the Roman Catholic lection from Wisdom 6:12–16.

Roman Catholics seem to be content with shorter readings than Episcopalians. Some of their readings were mere snippets, and we have therefore lengthened them. For example in Proper 10 in Year A the Old Testament reading (where the Roman reading, Isaiah 55:10–11) has been lengthened to Isaiah 55:1–5, 10–13. For some odd reason, when, in 1976, the eucharistic lectionary was changed into a "principal service" lectionary (*i.e.*, to be used whether the principal service is the Eucharist or Morning Prayer), this desire for longer lessons became more pronounced, and it is for this reason that optional lengthenings are provided in parenthesis; *e.g.*, Proper 6 in Year A, which reads: "Matthew 9:30–10:8 (9–15)." The supposition is that verses 9–15 would be used when the principal service is Morning Prayer, though there would be nothing to prevent the use of the longer selection at the Eucharist.

This brings us to another point. In the Roman lectionary, during the Easter season, the first Lesson is always from Acts. For the benefit of those parishes which have Morning Prayer as their main service, the Standing Liturgical Comission provided an alternative Old Testament reading. In that case, the Acts lesson should be read in the second position, where it is provided as the alternative selection. It was hoped that the clergy would get the point: the Acts reading is *always* meant to be read in the Great Fifty Days. Experience has shown, however, that clerics often miss the point, and carefully thread their way through the alternatives so as to avoid Acts—rubrical, no doubt, but not the way it was intended. Let us therefore gloss the rubric with an interpretation:

1. Always read Acts during the Easter season.

2. Only use the Old Testament reading if your principal service is Morning Prayer, in which case always drop the lesson from the Epistles or Revelation, but never drop Acts.

If this gloss is not followed, one may get such egregious liturgical crimes as omitting Acts 1:1–11 on Ascension Day!

## Towards an Ecumenical Lectionary

One of the hopes we had when we adopted the Roman lectionary was that it would become an ecumenical lectionary; *i.e.*, that the other Churches would follow suit and also adopt it. This has now actually happened to a gratifying extent. As well as Rome, Lutherans and Episcopalians use the lectionary with our respective modifications. We both do so regularly and faithfully, because our traditions have always been accustomed to the idea of a lectionary. Other mainline Protestant churches have made it available for optional use; *viz.*, the Methodist, Presbyterian, United Church of Christ, and the Consultation on Church Union. These denominations have traditionally been allergic to the idea of a lectionary, and many still are; but there is a steady growth in its use and in the appreciation of its advantages. It is a major ecumenical achievement that we are almost all listening to the same portions of Scripture Sunday by Sunday. Also, clerics of different traditions are meeting together in many places to prepare their Sunday sermons based on the lections.

The major impediment in this development has been the variations between the respective adaptations of the Roman lectionary. As a result, a few years ago the Consultation on Common Texts sponsored an ecumenical committee known as NACCL (North American Committee for Calendar and Lectionary), which has produced an ecumenically agreed lectionary. Its work is now complete, and it has been sanctioned for trial use in selected parishes of the Episcopal Church by the General Convention of 1982. One of the most novel features of the proposed revision is the change in the Old Testament readings for the period after Pentecost. Dissatisfaction has been expressed, especially by Old Testament scholars, with the restriction of Old Testament readings to predictions or typology matching the Gospels (see above). NACCL decided to stick to this procedure between Advent and Pentecost, where it is clearly appropriate. But after Pentecost a series of mini-courses of Old Testament readings has been proposed, six weeks in length each. Thus, it is proposed that there be a series on the patriarchs, the judges, the kings (David and Solomon), and the prophets (Elijah and Elisha), with selections from the prophetic writings in course. Then there will be a series of readings from the wisdom literature. We trust that this will meet the (certainly valid) criticism of the Old Testament scholars.

Less radical changes have been made in the New Testament and Gospel readings. NACCL's aim here was to insure that we all use the

8

same Gospel readings, however much we may vary on the other lections. Only minor textual arrangements have been made for the benefit of those Churches which use a lectern Bible, rather than printed lectionaries, in public reading.

Some lengthening of the New Testament pericopes has been made (*cf.* the remark about "snippets" above) and minor textual rearrangement to indicate the context of a particular reading. For example, apostolic greetings at the beginnings of the Epistles have been included, as well as other personal greetings and notices of local issues. Episcopalians will be gratified to discover that the proposed ecumenical lectionary has from time to time taken up precisely those modifications of the Roman lectionary which we have already made in our revisions. NACCL has endeavored to avoid the provision of alternative readings as much as possible. This has, however, been necessary where readings from the Apocrypha have been used. As already noted, some Churches have not been accustomed to readings from that source, and some have confessional barriers against its use. Modern scholarship, however, is breaking down the rather rigid distinction between the canonical and the apocryphal (deutero-canonical would be a better word), and it is to be hoped that the Churches of the Reformed tradition will eventually overcome their scruples about these writings and appreciate their value for public reading when used selectively.

All in all, it is to be hoped that the NACCL revision of the lectionary will be accepted. It will render the project even more serviceable to the cause of Christian unity than the earlier form of it has done in the past decade.

## BIBLIOGRAPHY

Borsch, F.H. *Introducing the Lessons of the Church Year: A Guide for Lay Readers and Congregations.* New York: Seabury, 1978.

Bushong, A.B. *A Guide to the Lectionary.* New York: Seabury, 1978.
> *Both the above serve a similar purpose. Concise statements of the subject matter for use in introducing the readings or in church bulletins.*

The Church Year. *Prayer Book Studies* 19. New York: The Church Hymnal Corporation, 1970.
> *The original publication of the Episcopal version of the three-year lec-*

*tionary. A preface states briefly the rationale of both Church Year and lectionary.*

Fontaine, G. *Commentarium ad Ordinem Lectionum Missae.* Vatican City: Typis Polyglottis Vaticanis, 1969.

*A commentary in French by the secretary of the Roman Catholic international committee which produced the Roman three-year lectionary.*

Fuller, R.H. *Preaching the New Lectionary.* Collegeville, MN: Liturgical Press, 1974.

*Contains interpretive commentary and homiletical suggestions. First appeared in Worship 1971–73 and designed for the Roman Catholic version of the lectionary. An index helps locate readings placed differently in the Episcopal form of the lectionary.*

*Interpretation* 31 (1977)

*Contains several articles on the three-year lectionary: Reumann, J. "A History of Lectionaries: From the Synagogue at Nazareth to Post-Vatican II" (pp. 116–30).*
*Sloyan, G.S. "The Lectionary as a Context for Interpretation" (pp. 131–38).*
*Bailey, L.R. "The Lectionary in Critical Perspective" (pp. 139–53).*
*Achtmeier, E. "Aids and Resources for the Interpretation of the Lectionary Texts" (pp. 154–64).*

*OrdoLectionum ProDominicis Feriis et Festis Sanctorum.* Vatican City: Typis Polyglottis Vaticanis, 1967.

*Sets out the Roman Lectionary and contains a brief preface in Latin stating its rationale.*

*Proclamation Commentaries.* Series 1 and 2. Philadelphia: Fortress Press, 1974 ff.

*The series of 64-page booklets, designed for ecumenical use by an ecumenical team of scholars, though giving preference to the Lutheran version of the three-year lectionary. The interpretive comments and homiletical suggestions are often by different authors.*

Reumann, J. (ed). *Studies in Lutheran Hermeneutics.* Philadelphia: Fortress Press, 1979.

*See especially the editor's essay, "The Lutheran Hermeneutics. An Overview and Personal Appraisal" (pp. 1–76) and A.J. Hultgren, "Hermeneutical Tendencies in the Three Year Lectionary" (pp. 145–73)*

10

Sloyan, G.S. *Commentary on the New Lectionary.* New Jersey: Paulist Press, 1979.

*Designed for the Roman Catholic lectionary by a reputable New Testament scholar.*

Sydnor, W. *Sunday's Scriptures: An Interpretation.* Wilton, CT: Morehouse-Barlow, 1976.

*Seeks to provide a common theme for each Sunday in the Episcopal version of the three-year lectionary.*

# The Passion of Witness: Prolegomena to the Revision of the Sanctoral Calendar

## The Reverend Thomas J. Talley
*Spring 1983*

## The Paschal Mystery

The Paschal Mystery, in which Christ the Lord passes through death upon the Cross and the sabbath of burial to rise in glory and ascend in triumph to the Father, constitutes the central idea (what Victor Turner calls the "root metaphor") of Christianity. In that passage, that process, that procession of symbols, all Christ's teaching achieves an historical realization, which the Church bears forward in the sacraments and in all her liturgical life. It is that Paschal Mystery which is at the heart of St. Paul's theology both of baptism and eucharist, and which early begins to shape as well the Christian ordering of time, of the week and of the year.

The annual celebration of "Pascha" prevents historical questions regarding its origins, which are still disputed; but the tendency of studies over the past two decades has been to reverse an earlier tendency, which saw that celebration as focused primarily on the resurrection of the Lord and to include his passion as hardly more than inherent in the resurrection story. More recently, it has appeared that the Christian year, as distinct from the Christian week, had its beginnings in more direct continuity with the Passover of the Law, being celebrated which a fast, vigil, and eucharist, stretching from the Preparation of the Passover, the 14th Nisan, through the night following, and ending around cockcrow on the day of Passover itself. According to the chronology of the passion in the Fourth Gospel, this one-day fast would coincide with the known date of the crucifixion, a factor which would deeply color the character of the Christian Pascha.

While the celebration of the Pascha was, like the Passover of the Law, a unitive celebration of our redemption in all its dimensions, writers of the Ante-Nicene period regularly (albeit inaccurately) spoke of the term *pascha* as being derived from the Greek verb *paschein*, to suffer, and so described the Pascha as celebration of the Lord's passion not of his resurrection. In contrast to the weekly celebrations of the Eighth Day, the first day of the new age inaugurated by the resurrection, the primitive Pascha marked the anniversary of the passion, which occasioned our redemption. This would remain true even after the conclusion of the fast was adjusted to the structure of the week so as to fall always on Sunday. So, for example, Origen could write in one of his Homilies on Isaiah:

> "There is now a multitude of people on account of the Preparation day, and especially on the Sunday which commemorates Christ's passion. For the resurrection of the Lord is not celebrated once in the year, but also always on the eighth day."

## Martyrs and Other Witnesses

While other factors would in time lead to many other sorts of festivals, among the very earliest liturgical commemorations were those of the days on which the martyrs perfected their witness to become sacraments of the Lord's passion. Like sacramental baptism, through which all Christians passed with the Lord through death and burial to new life in his Kingdom, the Kingdom of which the Church is sacrament, so "baptism of blood" was recognized as participation in the Lord's Paschal Mystery, such a sharing of his passion as would surely bring participation in his resurrection glory. This was the final act of perfect witness to Christ, the act by which the martyr testified to the Lordship of Christ over all history and the powers of history which occasioned his martyrdom.

While such a likening of martyrdom to the passion of the Lord can be seen already in the martyrdom of Stephen, it is from the passion of Polycarp, Bishop of Smyrna (A.D. 156), that we can first see the establishment of annual commemorative celebrations connected with the place of the martyr's burial. The very early accounts of Polycarp's martyrdom demonstrates perfectly that the Church of Smyrna understood the "political" event of their Bishop's execution as a liturgical event, which so perfectly exemplified a Pascha that it must become a day on which, each year, the Church would gather to remember and to make eucharist at his tomb. "There," the account says, "the Lord will permit us, so far as possible, to gather together in joy and gladness to celebrate the day of his martyrdom as a birthday, in memory of those athletes who have gone before, and to train and make ready those who are to come hereafter."

From such a second century tradition would develop the custom of observing the death dates of martyrs throughout the Church as the occasion of their heavenly birthdays (*natales*). While such commemoration would slowly be extended to include bishops and others whose lives gave exemplary witness to the Gospel of Christ, what is celebrated in every case is not the lives of accomplishments of the saints, but the historical completion of their baptism as they pass finally into the grave and gate of death, and through that into the Kingdom of the Lord, as that participation in Christ's paschal progress, which has opened the gate of heaven to all believers and made the death of his saints to be the ultimate witness to the power of the resurrection.

## From Local to Wider Commemoration

The New Testament speaks of all the baptized as saints, and nothing in the tradition of the Church would disavow that understanding. What is involved in sanctoral commemoration is not some "election" or "promotion" to sanctity, but the simple human fact that, while all the baptized are saints, some saints prove in time to be more memorable for some local churches than others. For that reason, it is not surprising to observe that such commemoration is at first quite local, since the memory of local leaders lives in the memory of the local community.

The earliest calendar at Rome, however, lists two days devoted to North African martyrs, in addition to the local Roman commemorations. This is usually understood to indicate the presence in Rome of a substantial community of North Africans, but it represents the beginning of an exchange of sanctoral commemorations between local churches, as communication led to a closer ecclesial community. The growth of such calendars of saints' days would lead eventually to synodical control and eventually to the notion of a "universal calendar," although not all those admitted to such a calendar have been celebrated in each place. The original principle of local veneration has lived on to produce variations in the sanctoral calendar from nation to nation, from religious order to religious order, and even from diocese to diocese. Indeed, those Holy Days observed most generally, those of biblical figures, are often among the later feasts introduced into the calendar. While some such observances are very ancient, the notion that each of the apostles and other figures prominent in the New Testament should be celebrated on an appropriate day represents a somewhat artificial development in the medieval period, valuable as it surely is for teaching.

Recent development in the custom of sanctoral commemoration has tended to reinforce the primitive element of local interest, and consequently more flexibility is encouraged. In the Roman Calendar, for example, not all commemorations listed are expected to be observed everywhere. Rather, as "optional memorials," their observance and the manner of it are left to local custom and authority. This leads as well, in our own tradition, to the liturgical commemoration of those who do in fact live in our historical memory as signs of God's grace at work.

Our concern in the formation of a sanctoral calendar is just that acknowledgement of the grace of God working in history, shaping it to his purpose through the lives which he has touched. While it would be strange to such a purpose to suppose that such a calendar could be, or should attempt to be, exhaustive, yet such a calendar has great value as a concrete expression of our memory.

We are faced, therefore, with the question of the *criteria* governing inclusion within such a calendar. The following are proposed:

1. *Historicity.* Saints' days are not celebrations of ideas that have been given mythical expression. Christianity is a radically historical religion and sees history as the locus of God's action. We should not, therefore, celebrate the lives of saints who are, in fact, only mythical figures. This does not, of course, preclude the liturgical celebration of theological or spiritual realities which are not presented as human lives within history.

2. *Christianity.* While the patriarchs and prophets of the Old Testament are a vital part of Christian history, and have been celebrated in various traditions, those included in a liturgical calendar should be identified with Christian history. For those who have lived within the Christian era, this will normally mean that they were baptized or that they suffered martyrdom while catechumens.

3. *Significance.* While no soul is insignificant, first attention should be given to those persons who seem particularly important for the contemporary life of the Episcopal Church, taking care that this contemporary life is understood as but one moment in the total history of the Catholic Church and the whole history of salvation.

4. *Historical Perspective.* From what historical viewpoint should such significance be assessed? Saving the possibility of more immediate local commemorations according to the Common of Saints, we propose that none be listed in the calendar before the passage of two generations from their death.

5. *Memorability.* Given such perspective, concern should be given both to holding the more memorable witnesses before the memory of the Church; and, on the other hand, recalling to the attention of the Church those whose memory may have faded in the shifting fashions of public concern but whose witness is deemed important to the life and mission of the Church.

While other criteria may be appropriate or needed, and while suggestions toward them are invited, these have been set forth as consistent with the theology of sanctoral commemoration which we have articulated and which we take to be fundamental to further development of our celebration of the victory of Christ, "in memory of those athletes who have gone before, and to train and make ready those who are to come hereafter."

## BIBLIOGRAPHY

Any summary of literature on the sanctoral calendar must, of course, give first place to the significant *Prayer Book Studies* which have already addressed the issue. PBS IX (1957) summarized the discussion of sanctoral commemoration since the Reformation, examined the principles of calendar construction and made proposals for the revision of the Prayer Book calendar. This was carried further in PBS XII (1958) which provided proper collects and readings for the proposed commemorations (these were printed out in full in a Supplement to Prayer Book Study XII in 1960). PBS XVI (1963) reviewed the work to that point, taking note of developments in other recent Anglican revisions and the revision of the Roman calendar, and proposed further alterations and additions to the Proper of Saints. These proposals were issued and approved for trial use as *Lesser Feasts and Fasts* in 1964. PBS XIX (1970) addressed the wider matter of the entire Church Year and Appendix I gave further consideration to the calendar, proposing a few new entries and the alteration of some dates. Appendix V of PBS XIX provides a rich bibliography of works on the liturgical year, including the sanctoral calendar, up to 1969.

To all that work, for which we are indebted to a great many but especially to the continuing hand of Dr. Massey H. Shepherd, some more recent titles can be added. In volume 50 of *Worship* (May, 1976, pp. 238–246) Richard Nardone presented an essay, "The Roman Calendar in Ecumenical Perspective," which reviews the recent work on that calendar and the problems presented by moving saints' feasts from their traditional dates. A fine article on "The Sanctoral" is provided by Kevin Donovan, S.J., on pp. 419–431 of *The Study of Liturgy* (Oxford, NY, 1978), edited by C. Jones, G. Wainwright, and E. Yarnold. This supplies another good bibliography and an additional note points to developments beyond the pre-Tridentine western tradition on which the body of the article is primarily and understandably focused. Another work on the Roman calendar is Adolf Adam, *The Liturgical Year* (Pueblo Publ. Co., NY, 1981), where chapter VIII is given to feasts of saints and pp. 224–248 focus on the rationale for the revisions made in the Roman calendar since Vatican II. *The Times of Celebration: Concilium 142*, edited by David Powe (Seabury Press, NY, 1981), is a collection of more wide ranging essays on liturgical time. Three of the essays (Talley, Cupungco, and Dalmais) touch to one degree or another on feasts of fixed date, including saints' days, and that of Dalmais is particularly concerned with the relationship between local calendars and the broader calendar of the Roman Church.

# The Liturgy in Easter Season

## Michael W. Merriman

*Spring 1984*

This period of the year, from Easter Day to the Day of Pentecost, is the oldest part of the Church Year. It is directly derived from the fifty-day period in the Jewish Calendar, which begins with Passover and ends with Pentecost (the Greek term for fifty days). The Lord's death and resurrection took place at Passover and the empowering of the apostolic Church by the Holy Spirit took place on Pentecost. In the Jewish Calendar, these days could fall on any day of the week, but in Christian tradition they were moved to the Sundays following because of the early Christian's intense reverence for the first day of the week as the Lord's Day, the Day of Resurrection. These were the Church's earliest festivals.

The early Christians also considered every Sunday to be a celebration of the rising of Christ and of the Holy Spirit—a weekly Easter and a weekly Pentecost.

At an early date the Great Fifty Days came to have a number of liturgical characteristics which set them apart from the remainder of the Church Year. Many of those were lost in later generations, but others are still very much a part of our liturgy, and some others have been revived by many of the liturgical churches in recent years. Some of the more notable of these Eastertide liturgical notes are described here.

*Alleluia.* This word, derived from the Hebrew word "Hallelujah," means literally "Praise Yahweh." In Jewish worship it is particularly characteristic of Passover. In the Seder meal the entire group of psalms called the "Hallel Psalms" are sung (Psalms 113 through 118). As a result, the Hallel Psalms themselves have been of particular importance in the Chistian passover, that is, Easter. (Note the use of Psalm 114 at the Easter Vigil.) As early as the time of the writing of the Book of Revelation, Hallelujah had an important place in the Church's worship, as can be seen in the description of the worship in heaven in that book. One notices in the liturgies during Easter Season that the word "Alleluia" is used not only in its usual places but also in many hymns and other parts of the liturgy.

*The Book of Acts of the Apostles.* This book, with its description of the life of the early Christian community, characterized by an intense awareness of the Risen Lord's presence and the apostolic preaching of the Resurrection, has had an important place in the Church's Easter liturgy. In recent years the liturgical revisions among Anglicans, Roman Catholics, Lutherans, and others have placed it again in the Easter liturgy. The Acts of the Apostles furnishes one of the readings every Sunday during the Great Fifty Days. (So important is this tradition that the Book of Common Prayer prescribes that if an Old Testament lesson is used in this season, Acts should be read as the second lesson.)

Other books of Scripture traditionally associated with Easter Season are the Gospel according to John, I Peter, I John, and the Book of Revelation. The Gospel readings in almost every case are from John. Each of the years in the three-year cycle of readings features one of the other three for the second reading at the Eucharist. For example, in Year C the readings are from Revelation. It is chosen because of its vision of the resurrected Church at worship as it praises its victorious Lord, which is an image of our worship, especially at the Eucharist.

*The Paschal Candle.* A large candle, first lighted at the Great Vigil on Easter Eve, burns in a prominent place (frequently near the pulpit or lectern from which the Gospel is proclaimed) at every service during the season. It was the custom of the Jewish synagogue to begin services in the evening with the lighting of candles—originally for the purpose of giving light, but almost immediately invested with the symbolic meaning of light: the revelation of God's love. Early Christians continued in that use of light, seeing in the bringing of light into a dark place a symbol of the Resurrection. As early as the fourth century, the celebration of the Resurrection in Jerusalem began with a candle lighted in the Holy Sepulchre and brought out during the night of Easter Eve to the words, "The light of Christ." That ceremony spread throughout the Christian Church many centuries ago.

The Paschal Candle (from the Latin word *Pascha,* which means Passover) is often decorated with five nails, which represent the wounds from the Crucifixion which the Risen Lord's body still bore. In ancient Christian basilicas, some of which still exist in Italy, the stand for the Paschal Candle was built into the pulpit as a permanent feature of the building's architecture. In the Middle Ages, Winchester Cathedral had a Paschal Candle which was sixty feet tall. In many places, out of Easter Season, it is kept near the font and is relighted for baptisms and funerals.

*Sunday themes in Eastertide.* Certain scriptural themes which highlight the meaning of the Resurrection have been part of the Church's tradition for many centuries. The Sunday after Easter Day (the second Sunday of Easter) always has as its Gospel reading the Risen Lord's appearance to Thomas. The theme is, of course, not "doubting Thomas," but Thomas' outburst of praise in which Jesus is first recognized as God ("My Lord and my God!", he said), and Jesus' words about us: "Blessed are those who have not seen and yet believe."

The Third Sunday of Easter in each year gives an account of a resurrection appearance in which Jesus eats with his friends. Its significance for Christians lies in its Eucharistic pattern. It was in the breaking of bread that Jesus was first recognized after his resurrection. It is in the breaking of bread in Eucharist that we encounter our risen Lord now; thus, our response at that point in the liturgy: "Alleluia. Christ our Passover is sacrificed for us. Therefore let us keep the feast. Alleluia."

The Fourth Sunday is called "Good Shepherd Sunday" because its Gospel reading always reflects Jesus' relationship to us in the image of the Good Shepherd: he who knows us by name, who provides for our needs, who saves us from evil, and who guides us into new life.

The Fifth Sunday has readings from John in which, prior to the Crucifixion, Jesus foretold the results of his death for the future of his followers. In Year A, his death will make him the way for us into eternal life: "I am the way and the truth and the life." In Year B, his death will prepare the way for us to receive the Holy Spirit, who will bind us into his life. In Year C, his death, as the ultimate expression of his love, will give us the model for Christian living: to love one another as he loved us.

The Sixth Sunday's Gospel readings have Jesus describing the result of our new life in him. Year A describes that life as a union between a vine and its branches: the branches draw their life from the vine. Year B reveals that the new life of divine love which we have received makes us no longer simply servants of God but friends of God. And in Year C we hear his promise that the Holy Spirit will be the source of our continued life in him and will be our Counsellor.

On the following Thursday, following Luke's chronology for our Lord's Ascension to the Father on the fortieth day after the Resurrection, we celebrate Ascension Day. This is not an event separable from the Resurrection, but one of three parts of one event: rising, ascending, and giving the Spirit. (The Prayer Book, p. 287, is clear that the Paschal Candle should not be extinguished on this day, but should continue to burn at all services through the Day of Pentecost.)

On the Seventh Sunday, the Sunday after Ascension Day, we hear each year a different portion of the "high priestly prayer" (John 17), the prayer that Jesus prayed on the night before his death for us: that the glory he has received from the Father may be given to us (Year A); that under the Father's protection we may have unity and become witnesses to the truth (Year B); and that our unity with each other in the Father and the Son may be a witness to the world (Year C).

Finally, the season of Easter is completed on the Day of Pentecost or Whitsunday. This celebrates the third action of Christ's victory over death: the gift of the Holy Spirit to the Church. In the first and second readings we have a wonderful juxtaposition of themes. The story of the Tower of Babel describes the result of the human attempt to reach God on our own, the breaking up of humankind into different language groups and ultimately the disunity of all people. The second reading, from Acts, shows the disciples waiting for God to reach out to them. Their waiting is rewarded by the coming of the Holy Spirit, which makes it possible for them to speak of the good news in the language of all peoples. God now is the source of reuniting the human race in Christ by the power of the Holy Spirit. The Gospel reading reveals that through the Holy Spirit we become the means for Jesus' ministry to continue. Receiving his peace, we become his instruments of that peace to the world. On this day the full results of redemption in the risen Lord come to light and are the cause of our celebration. In response, we keep this day as a baptismal day, and even if there are no candidates to be baptized or confirmed we are led in the renewing of our baptismal vows.

---

These Eastertide themes were old and hallowed as early as the fourth century when they were used by the Church to instruct the newly baptized in the "mysteries" of the faith. In those days, the unbaptized were not allowed to take part in the Prayers of the People, the exchange of the Peace, or the sacraments—especially the Eucharist—until after they were baptized. These readings and themes were used by the great teaching bishops of the fourth, fifth, and sixth centuries to reveal the meaning of those liturgical events.

The unbaptized were not allowed to take part in the Prayers of the People because, in the new covenant community of the baptized, we are ourselves the priesthood that comes directly to the Father in intercession, rather than depending on others to do that for us. In our own liturgical practice it is important to notice that it is not the leader of those prayers who does the praying; that person (whether ordained or not) simply announces the theme, and all of us, the baptized, royal priesthood, pray to the Father in the power of the Spirit.

The Peace is the greeting of the risen Christ. It is his invariable salutation in his resurrection appearances. We greet one another with *his* Peace. We are not merely being friendly, nor are we attempting to show our friends that we like them. We, the Body of Christ by virtue of our baptism, are bringing our risen Lord's presence to each other.

In Eucharist and the other sacraments, it is all the baptized, not just the clergy, who celebrate. Again our share in Christ's Priesthood is revealed. It is not simply bread and wine which are offered to God to be filled with Christ; the bread and wine are the signs and the bearers of those who offer them are his Body and Blood.

In Easter Season, those newly baptized, and all the baptized, have revealed to them the fullness of our redemption and the depth of our life in Christ. In the words of St. Augustine (preached to the newly baptized in his cathedral at Easter),

> "You are the Body of Christ. In you and through you the work of the Incarnation must go forward. You are to be taken. You are to be blessed and broken and distributed that you may be the means of grace and the vehicles of the eternal charity."

Alleluia! Christ is risen!
The Lord is risen indeed! Alleluia!

# Rites of Initiation

## The Reverend Charles P. Price
*September 1984*

The purpose of this paper is to clarify as much as possible some of the confusion surrounding the rites of initiation in the 1979 Book of Common Prayer. In particular it will examine the relation of Baptism to Confirmation and the rites for the reception of new members and the reaffirmation of baptismal vows. Certain practices will be recommended to secure consistency of administration throughout the Church.

## I.

1. The initiatory rite in BCP 1979 is the service of Holy Baptism. That rite comprises the following elements:

• Proclamation of the Word of God.
• Presentation and Examination of the Candidates.
• The Baptismal Covenant (basically the Creed).
• Thanksgiving over Water.
• Consecration of Chrism.(This element of the service is used only by the bishop.)
• The Baptism.

—Each candidate is presented by name.

24

—The celebrant or an assisting priest or deacon immerses each candidate or pours water on each one.

—The celebrant prays over the candidates, using a form of the prayer for the seven-fold gifts of the Spirit.

—The bishop or priest places a hand on the person's head, marking the forehead with a sign of the cross, using chrism if desired.

—The newly baptized are welcomed.

—The Peace is exchanged.

• The Eucharist may follow, although an alternative ending is provided. It must be recognized that circumstances may arise when the celebration of the Eucharist is impossible. Nevertheless, the Eucharist was anciently the climax and conclusion of the initiatory rite, and should be so regarded in BCP 1979.[1]

The service so outlined is the complete rite of initiation. Nothing else is *required* for full membership in the Church. The "confirmation rubric" of earlier English and American books, which stipulated that no one could be admitted to Holy Communion unless confirmed or "ready and desirous of being confirmed," has been dropped.[2]

2. In other words, Confirmation as it appears in BCP 1979 is not a prerequisite to communion. Baptized infants may receive the Eucharist. The recent experience of the Church with infant communion makes it increasingly clear that every argument against infant communion also counts against infant baptism. ("They aren't old enough to know what they're doing.") Conversely, all the arguments for infant baptism apply to the admission of the youngest children to the Lord's Table. ("Even the youngest are part of God's family.") The admission of young children to communion is a pastoral matter, to be worked out between parents and parish priest.[3] Basically it ought to be encouraged.

## II.

3. Little is known about the earliest baptismal liturgies. References in Acts[4] (ca. 75 A.D.), *Didache*[5] (ca. 100 A.D.), and Justin Martyr[6] (ca. 150 A.D.) seem to imply that baptism involved only water, probably poured over the candidates' heads, either "in the name of

the Lord Jesus Christ" or "in the name of the Father, and of the Son, and of the Holy Spirit."[7] Protestant Churches have returned to the New Testament for as much of their practice as possible. They insist that water-baptism alone is essential for full membership in the Church. It seems difficult to contest that position by appeal to a scriptural norm.

4. The first text known to us of a full baptismal liturgy comes from the *Apostolic Tradition of Hippolytus,* a document of the early 3rd century.[8] It is quite an elaborate service. It provides for thanksgiving over oil of thanksgiving, exorcism of oil of exorcism, renunciation of "Satan, and all thy servants, and all thy works," anointing with oil of exorcism by a presbyter, affirmation of a creed remarkably similar to the Apostles' Creed during Baptism in water, and anointing with oil of thanksgiving by a presbyter after the baptism. At the end, the bishop lays a hand on each of the candidates, anoints them again with oil of thanksgiving and signs them with a cross on the forehead. Most of these elements have been taken into the liturgy for baptism in the BCP 1979.

5. Although the service in Hippolytus is considerably more elaborate than the liturgy which can reasonably be inferred to lie behind the description in Acts, *Didache,* and Justin, the added elements contribute no new meaning. They emphasize and dramatize what is implied in water-baptism: the gift of the Holy Spirit,[9] membership in the royal priesthood of Christ,[10] and bearing his cross.[11] They do not add anything essentially new. Otherwise, the completeness of earlier baptisms would be called into question, and the Lord's institution of baptism itself might be deemed incomplete.[12]

6. In Eastern Orthodoxy a rite with elements analogous to everything found in Hippolytus—and more besides—persists to this day.[13] Presbyters, however, have been authorized to perform the whole service, including the last part, reserved in Hippolytus for the bishop. In Rome, on the other hand, and eventually throughout the western Catholic Church, presbyters were authorized to preside at the first part of the service but bishops retained control over the final ceremonies: laying on of a hand, chrismation, and consignation.[14] This last part of the service, which became separated in place and time from the first, was called, variously, *perfection* or *completion,* or *confirmation*.[15] After some time, it came to be regarded as a separate sacrament,[16] although the close connection with baptism

always remained. While one could receive communion without confirmation if in danger of death, and while such a person died in the communion of the Church, nevertheless that person's baptism was in some sense incomplete. One was expected to be "confirmed" or "completed" as soon as possible after baptism.[17]

7. Thus baptism without confirmation was an ambiguous act. Was it or was it not complete? And confirmation without baptism became, as someone has said, a rite in search of a theology. Did it confer the Holy Spirit in a different way? or did it represent, as came to be thought later, a rite of passage to maturity? All of these? In fact, possibly because of this lack of clarity, confirmation tended to fall into neglect during the Middle Ages. Even the best efforts of various local synods failed to enforce its use.[18] The "confirmation rubric" of earlier Anglican Prayer Books was devised in 1281, as is well-known, *to encourage confirmation, not to exclude from communion.*[19] Nothing short of this threatened excommunication had served that purpose; and, as things worked out, not even this drastic measure succeeded in bringing children to an early completion of their baptisms. Later medieval practice consequently tended to postpone confirmation until "years of discretion." Thomas Aquinas understood confirmation as a "sacrament of maturity," bringing an increase of grace for a different phase of life.[20] Yet even he argued that confirmation could be received by infants through the representation of their sponsors. When a bishop was present, baptism, confirmation, and communion continued to be administered to infants, in the ancient manner. Bishop Stokesly of London baptized Elizabeth Tudor when she was three days old, and Archbishop Cranmer confirmed her immediately afterward.[21]

8. Nevertheless, confirmation came more and more to be postponed, and the interval used for instruction. Baptism, first communion, and confirmation were all separated by appreciable intervals of time, though different arrangements prevailed in different parts of the world. In some regions (notably in Spain and hence parts of Latin America), confirmation still occurs immediately after baptism; but elsewhere it is usually postponed until the 4th or 7th year. The catechism of the Council of Trent speaks of "the age of reason."[22] On the Continent, first communion usually precedes confirmation.

After the Reformation, the Church of England accepted the late medieval fragmentation, with first communion coming after confirmation "at years of discretion," in accordance with the Sarum rubric of 1281. The term "years of discretion" has never been officially defined.

## III.

9. In view of the fact that both the practice and meaning of confirmation had become so hard to define, the first plan of the framers of the 1979 initiatory rite was to restore baptism to its ancient integrity and to eliminate confirmation as a separate service, on the Eastern Orthodox model. Such a rite was proposed in *Prayer Book Studies* 18 (1968), and in *Services for Trial Use,* 1970, where Holy Baptism appears much as it does in BCP 1979 under the title *Holy Baptism with the Laying on of Hands.*

10. The parts of the service following water-baptism in all three of these texts are *like* the confirmation service of earlier Anglican books, in that they begin with the prayer for the seven-fold gifts of the Spirit. Some form of this prayer has appeared in the *Confirmation* service of English and American Prayer Books since 1549 and in medieval Latin confirmation rites at least since the time of the Gelasian sacramentary, a document from the 8th century.[23] They also involve the laying of the celebrant's hand on the candidate. The use of oil, signing with the sign of the cross, and the formula of sealing with the Holy Spirit are part of the traditional pre-Reformation rite of confirmation. They are signs of the restored unity of the rite.

11. However, the parts of the service following water-baptism in these texts are *unlike* the older confirmation service, in that the minister of them may be a presbyter. As we have seen, in Eastern Orthodox Churches, presbyters have been the appointed ministers of the whole rite of baptism, including this part, from a very early time.

12. PBS 18 proved unacceptable. Although the confirmation service of earlier Anglican books, with some changes, had been restored to the liturgy for baptism, the new rite of initiation made no provision for commitment to Christ at the years of discretion. *For purposes of discussion we shall call the older confirmation service Confirmation A.* When Confirmation A became once more part of baptism, there was no opportunity for persons baptized as infants to confess

28

their faith in Christ as they reached an age of maturity and as faith developed, or to receive the strengthening of the Spirit at such a crucial time. To meet this need, *A Form of Commitment to Christian Service* was first proposed.[24]

13. Further discussion revealed that even this provision was not sufficient to meet the felt need. A service of public commitment and empowerment was called for, involving the participation of the bishop as the representative, in Episcopal polity, of the whole Church. Consequently, a more formal rite for mature commitment was proposed in 1973, including affirmation of baptismal vows and laying on of hands by the bishop. This new service was, by popular demand, called *Confirmation,* despite the possibility of misunderstanding. *For purposes of this discussion we shall call Confirmation as it appeared in 1973 and in BCP 1979 Confirmation B.*

14. Confirmation B is *like* confirmation in earlier Anglican Prayer Books, chiefly in that its minister must be a bishop. It also involves laying on of hands. The formula, "Defend, O Lord, this thy child..." associated with confirmation since 1552, may still be used, although an alternative formula is provided.

15. On the other hand, Confirmation B is *unlike* confirmation in earlier Anglican books in that it no longer includes the traditional prayer for the seven-fold gifts of the Spirit; and the laying on of hands, rather than the laying on of *a hand* is directed.[25] The formula, "you are sealed by the Holy Spirit in Baptism..." echoes the Orthodox formula for charismation at the end of baptism: "The seal of the gift of the Holy Spirit." Therefore, *it is the last portion of Baptism which more closely resembles confirmation in earlier Prayer Books* (Confirmation A).

The use of the title *Confirmation* to apply to *Confirmation B* is the chief source of ambiguity about the present initiatory rite.

16. As BCP 1979 took shape, the revisers realized the need for two other liturgical provisions, not covered in earlier English or American books: (1) for the reception of new members already baptized in other denominations and (2) for the reaffirmation of baptismal vows on the part of Episcopalians whose faith had undergone a significant deepening since confirmation. As in confirmation itself (Confirmation B), the appropriate action on the part of the candidates at such critical turning points in their lives is a reaffirmation

29

of baptismal vows, and the appropriate action on the part of the Church is a prayer for the renewing power of the Spirit, accompanied by some symbolic gesture on the part of the bishop in the name of the whole Church.

Therefore, these services were combined under the title, *Confirmation, with forms for Reception and for the Reaffirmation of Baptismal Vows* (BCP 1979, pp. 418–419). This material is also included within the service of Holy Baptism as a convenience, because it is likely to be used with Baptism at the bishop's visit. However, strictly speaking, Confirmation (Confirmation B), Reception, and Reaffirmation are not parts of Holy Baptism. Confirmation A *is* part of Holy Baptism.

17. The result of the evolution described in paragraphs 9–16 is an initiatory rite capable of at least two interpretations.

(a) Many Episcopalians, including a number of bishops, recognize no substantial change in the initiatory rites. As it always did, Christian initiation in BCP 1979 consists of Holy Baptism, Confirmation (here referred to as Confirmation B), and first communion. These elements appear in BCP 1979 as they have in every earlier English and American BCP. It is true that baptized persons may now be admitted to communion without confirmation; but confirmation is still the "expected" completion of baptism. The similarities between Confirmation B and the earlier rite of confirmation have been noted.

The elements which follow water-baptism in BCP 1979, this argument runs, are really no substitute for confirmation unless done by a bishop. If a presbyter baptizes, Confirmation B is required to complete baptism.

Those who interpret the provision of BCP 1979 in this way will expect confirmation to be administered *not only to "those baptized at an early age,"* but also to those baptized in other denominations who have not received episcopal laying on of hands, as well as those baptized in this Church as adults by presbyters.

By this interpretation, those who have received laying on of hands by a bishop (in apostolic succession) in another denomination will be *received,* as before, usually with a handshake.

Those who, having been confirmed, elect to reaffirm their baptismal vows will be acknowledged, *but not with laying on of hands.* No manual acts, it will be noted, are prescribed for Reception and Reaffirmation (BCP 1979, pp. 418–419).

In all this there is no change in practices heretofore virtually universal in the Episcopal Church. *This interpretation of BCP 1979 is possible, but it is not the one intended by those who prepared the rite.*

(b) Those who accept the intention of the revisers acknowledge that this liturgy for Holy Baptism 1979 has restored the primitive unity of baptism, confirmation, and first communion. The addition of the prayer for the seven-fold gifts of the Spirit, the provision for anointing (though optional), and the formula, "N., you are sealed by the Holy Spirit. . ." are the hallmarks of ancient confirmation. Confirmation A is the ancient sacrament, now placed in conjunction with water baptism, as it was anciently. Holy Baptism in BCP 1979 has again become the full and complete service which it was in Hippolytus, and which it still is in Eastern Orthodox Churches, where presbyters are the designated ministers of the entire rite. In BCP 1979, the celebrant is the bishop when present, "In the absence of a bishop, a priest is the celebrant and presides" at the whole service.

18. Those who interpret BCP 1979 in this latter way will treat Confirmation, Reception, and Reaffirmation as follows:

(a) All those baptized at an early age, even with the reassembled liturgy, are expected to be confirmed (Confirmation B) by the bishop. *Confirmation B is the rite of maturity needed when baptism and Confirmation A have been reunited.* Confirmation B should be administered at a later rather than at an earlier age. Admission to Communion no longer depends on it. It must be undertaken willingly and deliberately.

(b) *Adults baptized in the Episcopal Church should not be "confirmed."* For adults, baptism, which includes Confirmation A, is a mature profession of faith, an act complete in itself.

(i.) Adults baptized by a presbyter should publicly *reaffirm their baptismal vows* before the bishop, and receive laying on of hands in order to establish symbollically their tie to the whole Church. The appropriate prayer is the one for Reaffirmation of Baptismal Vows. That is to say, the rubric which requires adults baptized by a presbyter to receive laying on of hands (BCP 1979, p. 412) may be complied with by using *laying on of hands as the bishop's manual act for Reaffirmation*. As noted previously, no manual act is specified.[26]

(ii.) Adults baptized with the laying on of a hand by a bishop (Confirmation A), require no further liturgical act.

(c) Adults baptized in other Churches who wish to become members of this Church do so canonically by having their baptisms duly recorded in this Church.[27] We acknowledge baptism in water in the name of the Trinity as the sole requirement for membership in this Christian community. (See para. 3.)

(d) It must then be ascertained in pastoral conversation with such adults whether they have made a mature commitment to Christ. If they have not, and if they have been baptized in infancy, they are expected to be confirmed by the bishop (Confirmation B).[28] This confirmation is *in no sense* a completion of baptism, but represents, as for Episcopalians baptized in infancy, the occasion of a mature commitment to Christ in the presence of a representative of the universal Church; and it provides renewing of the Spirit through prayer and the laying on of hands.

(e) If adults baptized in another church have already made a mature commitment to Christ in their former denomination, *they should be received by the bishop.* The appropriate manual act for the reception of new members from any denomination —whether Roman Catholic, Orthodox, Lutheran, or Baptist— is the laying on of hands, to symbolize that special link to the whole Church which our bishops represent to us. Such adults also receive strengthening power of the Spirit through prayer and the laying on of hands. The appropriate formula is that for Reception.

(f) Confirmed adults—or those received from other Communions—who experience a deepening of faith to which they wish to give public witness, may reaffirm their baptismal vows before a bishop and receive the laying on of hands in blessing, with prayer for the Spirit. This act may occur more than once.

(g) When laying on of hands is used in connection with all three of these rites—Confirmation, Reception, and Reaffirmation—it not only expresses a parallel and equal prayer for renewal in each case, but has the further advantage of securing the following desirable result: that whether a person comes into the fellowship of the Episcopal church under the traditional interpretation of the initiatory rite or under the interpretation suggested in this paragraph, he or she will receive the episcopal laying on of hands with prayers for the gift of the Spirit.

(h) The use of chrism in connection with the three rites associated with Confirmation B is not appropriate.

20. The use of chrism at confirmation (*i.e.*, Confirmation A) is ancient, and its symbolism complex. The biblical roots of the use of oil can be readily traced.[29] Oil represents the rich, flowing life of the Spirit.[30] It also suggests the anointing of the kingly and priestly people of God.[31] It lost its symbolic power for Churches of the Reformation, including the English Church. Its use was dropped in English and American Prayer Books after 1552.[32] Whether it will be generally regained under the present provision for optional use is uncertain. It is, in any case, improper to insist that it constitutes an *essential* symbol of the presence of the bishop at presbyteral baptism, when the priest lays a hand on the candidates and signs them with the sign of the cross. It may, of course, be taken to represent the bishop's presence in that action, since it can only be consecrated by him. That level of meaning, however, was late to develop. Moreover, the presbyter on whom the bishop has laid hands at ordination is an even better symbol of the bishop's presence (because personal) than oil which the bishop has consecrated.

*Although the use of oil may be regarded by some as enriching the initiatory rite, its use cannot be regarded as indispensible, nor may a baptism be performed by a presbyter without it being regarded as incomplete.*

## NOTES

1. BCP, pp. 299–311. *Cf.* Whitaker, E. C., *Documents of the Baptismal Liturgy*, pp. 4–7 (Ap. Trad. of Hip.); pp. 142–147 (Ambrosian Manual); pp. 186–190, *Gelasian Sacramentary*; p. 247 (Sarum Rite).

2. BCP 1928, p. 299. BCP 1549, Everyman's Library, J.M. Dent, London, 1949; p. 251. BCP 1552, op. cit., p. 409. It is well known that the same rubric has appeared in every intervening English and American Prayer Book. The phrase "ready and desirous of being confirmed" was added in 1662 to accomodate both those who had not been confirmed during the Commonwealth and those who lived in the new colonies. The mitigation implies that confirmation is not essential. In this case, it is maturity of faith which is required.

3. *Cf.* Price, C.P., *Liturgy for Living.* Seabury, 1979; pp. 103f. Holmes, Urban T., *Young Children and the Eucharist,* Seabury, 1972.

4. Acts 8.36; 10.47; 16.33, among others. These are the clearest references.

5. *Didache* vii.i, 3.

6. Justin Martyr, I Apology 61.

7. Acts. 2.38; Matthew 28.19. Also *Didache* vii.1, 3; ix.5.

8. *Apostolic Tradition of Hippolytus,* Part II, para. 21-23.

9. John 3.5; for sealing with the Spirit, *cf.* Ephesians 1.13.

10. I Peter 2.9.

11. Romans 6.34. *Cf.* Mark 8.34-35.

12. Matthew 28.19. This passage is cited as the institution of baptism by the risen Lord. It at least makes no explicit mention of liturgical actions in addition to water-baptism. In Jesus' own baptism, moreover, the coming of the Spirit, in the closest association with John's act ("straightway" according to St. Mark), involved no other liturgical act, but the sovereign freedom of the Spirit. For the essential unity of early baptismal liturgies, *cf.* Lampe, *Seal of the Spirit,* pp. 157f.

13. Schmemann, Alexander, *Of Water and the Spirit,* passim. The whole book is an exposition of the rite of baptism in the Greek Orthodox Church.

14. Although bishops retained control of these ceremonies in western catholicism, they always could authorize priests to perform them. Only under Anglican discipline has confirmation been so rigorously maintained as a prerogative of bishops only. *Cf. New Catholic Encyclopedia,* vol. 4, p. 149 (b).

15. Fisher, J.D.C., *Bapt. in Med. West,* pp. 141ff; also, Lampe, *Seal of the Spirit,* 174; also, Fisher, J.D.C., *Confirmation Then and Now,* pp. 126–9.

16. *Cf.* Lampe, *op. cit.* p. 179. Lampe places this development in the third century. It is one of the sacraments listed by Hugh of St. Victor (cf. Leeming, B., *Principles of Sacramental Theology,* Longmans, 1956, p. 566) and appears as one of the seven sacraments finally identified by Peter Lombard and Thomas Aquinas. (*Summa Theologica* 3a.72.)

17. Fisher, J.D.C., *Confirmation Then and Now,* pp. 127ff. The restriction of communion to those in danger of dying was soon lifted. Nevertheless, the question about the importance of confirmation continued to be asked. *Cf.* Fisher, J.D.C., *Christian Initiation: Baptism in the Medieval West,* pp. 20–21.

18. Fisher, J.D.C., *Bapt. in Med. West,* pp. 120–124.

19. *E.g.* Stevick, Daniel B., *Holy Baptism, Supplement* to PBS 26, p. 29.

20. Aquinas, *Summa Theologica* 3a.72.8.

21. Ridley, J., *Thomas Cranmer,* Clarendon Press, Oxford, 1962; p. 70.

22. *Cf. New Catholic Encyclopedia,* Vol. 4, p. 149 (b); McCormack, A., *Christian Initiation,* p. 98. There are indications that even in Latin America, confirmation practice is coming to conform to that of the rest of western catholicism.

23. *Cf.* Whitaker, E.C., *Documents of the Baptismal Liturgy,* SPCK, London, 1970; p. 188. Some scholars would place the origin of this prayer at an even earlier date. The phrase occurs in a prayer apparently used in this place in the liturgy discussed by St. Ambrose in *De Sacramentis* (4th century). *Cf.* Lampe, p. 208.

24. BCP, pp. 420–1; STU, pp. 326–7.

25. It would be a mistake to make too much of the earlier service of confirmation with the laying on of *a* hand, rather than the laying on *of hands.* In the Prayer Book tradition, the service of Confirmation had

no subtitle until 1662, when *The Laying on of Hands* appeared. However the rubric directing the bishop's action involved a singular "hand" from 1549–1662. In American Books, the subtitle *Laying on of Hands* was first used in 1789, 1892, and 1928; the rubric was also in the plural in the first two American books. In 1979, the singular form "hand," goes with the end of baptism; the rubric in Confirmation B reads "hands." This fact may be taken as an indication of the revisers' intentions, although the point must not be pressed to the point of saying that Confirmation A, done with two hands, is somehow improper.

26. *Cf.* paragraph 17.

27. Canon Title I, 16.1(a).

28. Canon Title I, 16.1(c).

29. Mitchell, Leonel L., *Baptismal Anointing*, SPCK, London, 1966.

30. *E.g.*, Isaiah 61.1.

31. Revelation 1.6; Leviticus 8.10 (for priests); I Samuel 16.13 (for the messianic king of David's line).

32. *Cf.* BCP 1549, Everyman's, p. 241, connected with *baptism*.
BCP 1552, Everyman's, p. 398 (baptism), p. 408 (confirmation).

It is at least arguable that Cranmer intended the baptism liturgy of 1549 to be a reunited service. Not only was the use of oil directed in 1549, but the language of the prayer used at the consignation in the 1552 service of baptism—the language of the Christian soldier—is *confirmation* language, as Marion Hatchett has argued. If Cranmer indeed intended to reunite baptism and confirmation, however, it must be acknowledged that the point was universally overlooked until the present round of revisions.

## BIBLIOGRAPHY

These are a few of the books which have been influential in shaping the discussion which lies behind this paper:

Dix, Gregory. *The Theology of Confirmation in Relation to Baptism.* Dacre Press, Westminster, 1946.
    *A brief statement of the position identified in this paper as traditional.*

Fisher, J.D.C. *Christian Initiation: Baptism in the Medieval West.* SPCK, London, 1965.

_____. *Christian Initiation: The Reformation Period.* SPCK, London, 1970.

_____. *Confirmation Then and Now.* SPCK, London, 1978.

*Three Alcuin Club Monographs which survey this question with depth and a wealth of scholarly references.*

Kavanagh, Aidan. *The Shape of Baptism: The Rite of Christian Initiation.* Pueblo, New York, 1978.

*A Roman Catholic Study in the light of Vatican II decisions.*

Lampe, G.W.H. *The Seal of the Spirit.* 2nd ed., SPCK, London, 1976.

*A thorough examination of the patristic development, whose conclusions tend to the revisionist position identified in this paper.*

McCormack, Arthur. "Christian Initiation," *Twentieth Century Encyclopedia of Catholicism.* Hawthorne Books, New York, 1969.

Schmemann, Alexander. *Of Water and the Spirit.* St. Vladimir's Press, 1974

*An exposition of the Greek Orthodox rite of initiation.*

Stevick, Daniel B. *Holy Baptism, together with A Form for the Affirmation of Baptismal Vows with the Laying-on of Hands by the Bishop, also called Confirmation,* Supplement to Prayer Book Studies 26, Church Hymnal Corporation, New York, 1973, revised 1987.

*An historical and theological exposition of the rite of initiation as proposed by the Standing Liturgical Commission in 1973.*

Thornton, Lionel. *Confirmation, Its Place in the Baptismal Mystery.* Dacre Press, Westminster, 1954.

*An ampler study than Dix's, from roughly the same point of view.*

Whitaker, E.C., ed. *Documents of the Baptismal Liturgy,* 2nd ed. SPCK, London, 1970.

*This useful volume contains original texts concerning baptism—liturgical, canonical, theological—from the* Didache *to the Sarum Rite.*

# The Power and the Promise of Language in Worship: Inclusive Language Guidelines for the Church

The Reverend Robert A. Bennett

*October 1984*

## I. The Power and the Problem of Language in Worship

Worship is not only the natural response to the reality of God within life; it is also one of the primary means whereby God touches us in order to transform us. The language we use in worship is therefore a vital medium in this most important occasion for encountering the living God. The very words used to articulate what we believe about God and who we believe God to be, plus what we believe about ourselves as a redeemed community, can themselves contribute to the power and the promise of this sacred time or they can detract from it and become a problem. The thoughts about language and the guidelines for Church use in this Occasional Paper are offered in the conviction that God would use our very speech so that the whole worshiping community may know the power and the promise of new life in Christ.

The words we speak are not just tools to express our thoughts. They are powerful shapers of who we are and of the world in which we live. Both aspects of this dual reality of speech are seen in the biblical doctrines of creation and redemption:

> "And God said, 'Let there be. . .' And it was so." (Genesis 1)
> "And the Word became flesh and dwelt among us. . ." (John 1)

The language of our culture, in which the divine revelation is expressed, also influences our grasp of God's intention for creation and humanity. From ancient times down into the present, the cultural context of the Judeo-Christian heritage has been male-oriented, and this patriarchal way of viewing reality has affected the way we perceive God and one another. Thus, much of the God-language in the Bible uses male-related terms to describe God's creative and saving activity. Masculine nouns and pronouns are used to designate the transcendent deity as well as the human actors in the story of the old and the new covenental communities of faith.

This cultural overlay in Scripture is further reinforced by our English translators, whose own male-centeredness and patriarchal bias leads them to add words even more male-gender-specific than are found in the original texts themselves. Numerous words in the original Hebrew and Greek, which grammatically may be either feminine or masculine, are regularly rendered as masculine in English Bible translations. The Greek word *tis,* for example, means "someone" or "anyone," but in the King James and Revised Standard Versions it is rendered as "any man," as in Mark 4:23, "If any man has ears to hear. . .", or John 7:17, "If any man will do his will. . ." Sometimes, translators introduce male references which are not found in the original. The Greek text of 2 Corinthians 5:17, for example, which has neither subject nor verb, is translated, "If any one is in Christ he is a new creation." Here, the Jerusalem Bible and New English Bible are more accurate in their rendering, "If any one is in Christ there is a new creation."

A similar shaping of an all-male reality, reflective of our cultural context, occurs within the language of the Anglican liturgical tradition. Fuller discussion of this particular phenomenon will follow below.

Theology, our ordered discourse about God, no less than Scripture and culture, is a powerful shaper of reality. Our God-language not only expresses what the community of faith thinks about God, but effectively forges the images of God for us and conditions how we relate to one another as people of faith. Much of our theological language shows the effect of transposing the biblical witness into the idiom of Greco-Roman philosophy and culture. The language of the creeds, for example, attempts to express Scriptural proclamation as mediated through the ongoing experience of Christ in Church tradition.

It is in the liturgical life of the Church today that all these powerful shapers of reality converge and come into play—Scripture, culture, theology and tradition. They are obviously more than mere tools for expressing what is, since within the powerful matrix of worship they merge and shape a new reality for us. And yet, intertwined with this promise of that which is new and renewing, there is also the problem of successive layers of male-oriented culture which suggest that God is male—and a white male at that—and that the redeemed are all male as well.

Language should be able to express the truth of God's creative and redemptive work, but language which is so male-oriented fashions a world which today makes many people feel excluded from this salvation proclamation. The problem of language in worship, therefore, stems from its very power and promise to shape who we are and what we can hope to become.

The liturgical tradition of the Episcopal Church is a particularly effective determiner of what Episcopalians believe about God and about themselves. Our task today, now that language is increasingly recognized as possessing such power, is to find ways of freeing the liberating word of Scripture and the Christ-experience so that they can more fully exert their saving and life-giving power within worship. Anglican liturgical tradition has a particularly difficult task to

40

deal with in the area of language, since English has been its vernacular for so long. Roman Catholic tradition, on this count, has had the advantage, within the Latin of the liturgy, of more precise terminology, such as *homo* for humanity and *vir* for male, and thus is more ready to tackle inclusive language issues in its new English texts.

Anglican Prayer Book tradition has for centuries let "man" carry the freight both for humanity and for male, and under the weight of long tradition is less ready to make changes in its language. Now that the term "man" has lost its generic meaning for large segments of society, change is needed if our worship is to continue to be a positive force in the lives of both men and women.

## II. Language in the Liturgy

The male bias of patriarchal assumptions—male as superordinate and female as subordinate, male as representative of the species and female as a subspecies—has been under attack by linguists, educators, child psychologists and book publishers for many years now. The National Council of Teachers of English, for example, published in 1975 its own set of *Guidelines for Nonsexist Use of Language* in NCTE Publications. These groups have recognized that male nouns and pronouns no longer carry a generic force within the English language for a growing number of people and should no longer be used to include female as well as male referents.

The churches have also begun to respond to this situation by establishing guidelines for helping the language of worship to express the joy of the inclusion of all persons in Christ. Inclusive language guidelines have been produced, for example, by the Roman Catholic, Lutheran and Presbyterian Churches. The Revised Standard Version of the Bible, as well, is being revised so as to limit the bias of translation in which male terms have been used for feminine or neutral terms in the original Hebrew and Greek. The National Council of Churches has produced an experimental *Inclusive Language Lectionary*. Here the sunday lessons have been recast—it is not a new translation—into more inclusive terms. Indeed, some of these very issues were already addressed in the language of Rite Two in the 1979 Book of Common Prayer and in its Psalter.

Despite its own culturally conditioned patriarchal bias, the Bible proclaims the equality of male and female before God and the gift of redemption as open to all. The Old Testament acknowledges that both male and female have been created in the image of God (Genesis 1:27). The New Testament witness of Paul, even though he was very much a child of his culture, is that our baptism in Christ means that our redeemed humanity can no longer recognize any form of superordination or subordination. He writes,

"There is Neither Jew nor Greek, there is neither slave nor free, there is neither male nor female; for you are all one in Jesus Christ." (Galatians 3:28)

Some examples point to the Church's recognition of the language problem within worship. recently, Roman Catholic bishops voted to change one of the English texts for the Mass prepared by the International Committee on English in the Liturgy (ICEL) to avoid exclusionary language. At the Words of Institution, instead of the Blood of Christ being "shed for you and for all men so that sins may be forgiven," it will now read "for you and for all so that. . ." The Book of Common Prayer, Morning Prayer, Rite Two, also recognizes this type of problem when it reads, in the General Thanksgiving (p. 101), "to us and to all whom you have made," in place of Morning Prayer, Rite One (p. 58), "to us and to all men." Similarly, the Gloria in Excelsis, Rite Two (p. 356), reads "and peace to his people on earth" in place of the Rite One (p. 324) "on earth peace, good will towards men."

As many young people hear "men" language, not as generic, but as male-specific and excluding females, so increasing numbers of adults acknowledge that they too hear such language as exclusionary, and in the context of worship are pained that the community of faith should countenance it. Not only females, but males as well, long for language which more precisely addresses them in worship as equal parts of humanity, and not as if one were superordinate and the other subordinate, or, as linguists point out, as if male is taken as the species and female as the subspecies. Such usage is not conducive to worshipful praise of the God who created male and female equal in the image of God, nor of the way we should view and relate to one another. Language shapes who we are as much as it expresses what we think of ourselves. The liturgy, as the prime arena in which we encounter the living God and engage one another as the household of the redeemed, must be faithful to the liberating word that emerges even out of the patriarchal language of the Bible and tradition.

Since we acknowledge our being made in the image of God, our anthropology informs our theology; our view of humanity informs our view of God. Change in language usage forces upon us, therefore, a corresponding change in expressing who we are as human beings and how we relate to one another, as well as in expressing who we believe God to be. The power and the problem of language today is that the Word made flesh in Christ demands that we be responsible in our use of language both about one another and about God. If we are open to such a demand, then we can talk instead about one another and about God. If we are open to such a demand, then we can talk instead about the power and the promise of language. The humanity of Jesus, which Christians believe to be a sign of what God intends for redeemed humanity, redefines how we are to treat one another.

Jesus calls us to move beyond cultural patterns of dominance and powerlessness as the key to defining relationships. These social configurations have been used as a theological justification for making God a dominant male master over subservient human subjects. Yet this caricature does not correspond to the biblical revelation nor to the resurrection witness of the Church. Women (no less than men, for example) followed Jesus, learned from him, and were the first to witness to the resurrected Christ. They too, therefore, bear the marks of discipleship. This reality, no less than the obvious fact that females as well as males share fully in God's redemption, needs to be expressed more clearly, precisely, and lovingly in contemporary liturgical speech. The liturgy celebrates that in Christ we are all truly brothers and sisters and no longer servants but children and heirs of divine promise.

## III. Language About Ourselves in Liturgy

Language usage in the Elizabethan Prayer Book and the King James Bible reflect 16th and 17th century cultural patterns which no longer correspond to how men and women relate to one another. In the same way that old patterns of 18th and 19th century black-white racial relations are no longer acceptable, so worship, as a living, dynamic encounter between God and humanity, must express where we are today in redeemed male-female relationships. The first priority of language in liturgy today is to make it more truly inclusive of all who call upon God's name in worship. This is not an easy task for Anglicans because the vernacular has been the speech which has shaped our cultural as well as our religious identity. It is also difficult to change old patterns and traditional ways of referring to one another. Our Roman Catholic sisters and brothers come relatively new to English as their worship idiom and hence do not have so much baggage of tradition; nevertheless, they and we struggle together to make liturgy truly expressive of its underlying liberating spirit of empowerment for all God's children.

How is this to come about when we have only recently and with much pain brought our 1979 Book of Common Prayer into use? The several inclusive-language changes in Rite Two are a beginning, as are the revised texts in *The Hymnal 1982*. But Prayer Book texts and hymns are only part of religious language. Other areas also need to be addressed. These are preaching, biddings and free prayer, religious education, and Scripture itself. The problems of our human-to-human discourse must be addressed immediately and this can take place right now in how we speak to and about one another. The following guidelines make specific suggestions about such changes that can be made in sermons, free prayer, biddings and announcements, and Christian Education material.

The scriptural problem is more difficult, given the pull of tradition and the fear of "tampering" with the biblical text. Yet scholars are beginning to face their own translation bias which has already "tampered" with the text in using male nouns and pronouns which do not occur in the Greek original. Despite the many objections to it, the National Council of Churches' *Inclusive Language Lectionary* is an attempt to make the liturgy truly more inclusive and more precise in the reading of the Bible.

## IV. Language About God in Liturgy

God-language—the terms used for God and the risen Christ—reflects our self-conception. Our theology and christology are influenced by our anthropology. While a change in attitude is needed to start the work of making our human-talk in liturgy more inclusive, an even more profound change is needed so that our ways of viewing God will not be exclusionary or limit our grasp of God's all-encompassing love.

Theologically speaking, God as father is a metaphor used to express something of the relationship between creator and creature, between transcendent deity and human beings in history. The Hebrew Bible, whose chief focus is Israel's encounter with the transcendent God, only sparingly uses such familial relationship terms, for fear of gross anthropomorphism—the idolatry of recreating God as a human being—and for fear of making God subject to ritual manipulation, as in pagan religions. The holiness of God is a more important Old Testament image for God, one which acknowledges God as transcendent, but also as the ultimate moral factor in life, as witnessed in the covenant between Holy God and holy people. For all of the patriarchalism of Hebrew male centeredness, God was never looked upon as a man:

"For I am God and not man (*lo'-ish*)." (Hosea 11:9b)

By the same token, the Old Testament was not afraid to speak of God in direct feminine metaphor, even as it fervently denied that God could have a female consort, as in polytheistic mythology:

"As one whom his mother comforts, so will I comfort you; you shall be comforted in Jerusalem." (Isaiah 66:13)

In the New Testament, Jesus makes a radical departure from Jewish tradition when he teaches us to call God "father" in the Lord's Prayer, fundamentally a parable teaching the accessibility of the transcendent and holy God. Jesus is saying, pray to the God of the Universe as one whom you can address as Abba ("daddy").

It is the intimate personal aspect, not the masculine one, which is stressed in this key discourse. Perhaps no greater problem faces us in worship than imaging God as a male patriarch, using masculine pronouns to refer to the subject of divine activity. When we say, "God the Father, he . . .", we too easily reduce that personal metaphor so characteristic of Jesus to literal patriarchal language. This symbol of the accessibility of God has become at this point, for increasing numbers of persons, exclusionary. Such a development is as serious a theological problem as it is an inclusive language one.

45

The metaphor of God as father, taken literally, changes into what has been forbidden—an idol.

## V. Language About Jesus and the Holy Spirit in the Liturgy

The christological problem is even more complex since Jesus was a male human being. The incarnation, however, stresses Jesus' humanity in relation to God, not his maleness. The Greek word behind the credal affirmation is anthropos, meaning "human being," and not "man" as a male person. While we must be faithful to the historical reality of Jesus as a man, Jesus' christological or divine/human function includes and goes beyond his maleness to encompass all humanity. There is an increasing call to stress the humanity of Jesus rather than his maleness and to focus on the resurrected humanity of the Christ into which we can all be baptized without obliterating our sexual identities.

The Trinitarian doxologies in the collects and prayers stress the internal relatedness of the triune God. But these come forth as an overly masculinized three-in-one God, which is one of the root causes of women's feeling of oppression in the liturgy. Since our thinking about the Holy Spirit is not so rigidly fixed, the resulting fluidity of images and language about this Person of the Trinity may well be the basis for discovering new insights and inclusive designations for the three-in-one Godhead. The Holy Spirit conveys both the sense of God's creative activity toward us and the sense of divine power moving through us, and thus has been characterized as more a depth-dimension than a dimension of transcendence. As we seek to uncover the power and the promise of language within worship, this more "impersonal" element within the Trinity may be that depth-dimension which can lead to non-exclusive relational language about God and Jesus Christ.

## VI. Guidelines for Inclusive Language in Church Life

A first priority is the correcting of obviously limiting terminology which excludes women from feeling that they are part of the worshiping community. The Standing Liturgical Commission, of course, has no authority to propose ad hoc changes in The Book of Common Prayer, but it does recommend that wherever possible in sermons, readings, prayers and especially within free prayers that are possible in the Prayers of the People, in Christian Education materials, in parish bulletins, and in meetings, ministers and congregation should be sensitive to the power of language to shape reality and to be either a deadly weapon or a channel of healing grace.

## A. Language About Ourselves

In order to remedy the male bias of our liturgical language as well as our general speech, care should be taken to use phrases which include women and are more theologically accurate and just. The language problem arises when women are excluded or demeaned and when persons are stereotyped in any form. Thus, care and effort should be made to find alternative words, phrases and grammatical constructions which affirm personhood, as well as learning to avoid those things in our speech which deny it. Some suggested alternatives which include and thus affirm are:

| Inclusive | Excluding |
|---|---|
| All, humankind | Man, mankind |
| Ancestors, forebears | Forefathers |
| Children of God | Sons of God |
| Companion, friend, community | Brother, Bretheren |
| Communion | Fellowship |
| One, one who, they; their | He, him; his |
| Presiding Officer, Chair | Chairman |

In order to avoid excessive use of male pronouns, make fuller use of proper names, or of plural pronoun forms; or rephrase the sentence so as not to have to use gender-specific forms. Recast your speech into second-person direct address, as an alternative to third-person reference, or take care to include female as well as male references.

When addressing groups, use expressions which create a feeling of equality as well as inclusivity. Couples, for example, should be addressed as "John and Mary Smith," rather than "Mr. Smith and his wife" or "Mrs. Smith and her husband." Note that the phrases "husband and wife" or "man and woman" place the two persons on an equal footing, which the too-often-heard "man and wife" does not.

Needless to say, sensitivity in gender-related matters must also carry over into language which refers to other Churches or faiths,

47

races, social groups, or nations. Do not use expressions such as "deaf and dumb" or "the afflicted," since these are offensive abstractions which exclude and mark persons and groups as defective. Avoid using color symbolism which equates light and white with positive values while consigning dark and black to negative ones.

Eliminating excluding and demeaning language may not eliminate sexist or racist conduct, but as language is freed from such usage and assumptions, women and men can begin to share more fully in the gift of worship and the promise of new existence.

## B. Language About God

God-language as fixed by tradition, is more difficult to change. Nevertheless, every effort should be made to relieve the preponderance of masculine usages in the free prayers which are part of the Prayers of the People. Yet not only in these prayers, but in all the other contexts mentioned above, masculine pronouns for God should be replaced with the word "God," or else sentences with the objectionable sequence "God...he...he...his" should be recast so as to avoid such sequences. There is a rich reservoir of divine names from Scripture, tradition, and hymnody which can be tapped for alternatives. Psalm 18 ( = 2 Samuel 22), for example, has no less than ten such alternative names, all with the possessive attached so as to indicate close personal relationship: My Rock; My Stronghold; My Deliverer; My God; My Mountain; My Suzerain; The Horn of My Salvation; My Redoubt; My Refuge; My Savior.

"I love you, O LORD (YAHWEH) my strength,
 O LORD my stronghold, my crag and my haven.
My God, my rock in whom I put my trust,
 my shield, the horn of my salvation and my refuge;
 you are worthy of praise." (Psalm 18:1-2, BCP p. 602)

The term "Lord" is increasingly felt to be excluding because in English it is gender-specific, as in the phrase "lords and ladies," while its equivalent, "Sovereign," is not. Thus also, the words King, Kingdom, and Kingship, used of God and of Jesus, have non-excluding equivalents in Ruler, Realm, and Reign. Remember that on the lips of Jesus, "Father" is another way of saying that the Holy and transcendent deity is a personal, loving God and can be compared to a caring parent. By the same token, the affirmation that Jesus Christ is the Son of God loses nothing in its direct equivalent "Child of

48

God," which can be found in such key early Christian writers as Chrysostom and Hippolytus. Indeed, the term "child" as applied to Jesus is characteristic of the very early Christian text,

> "which you have revealed to us through Jesus your Child." (*The Didache*)

Though they may sound strange initially, the following suggested God-language changes are accurate, in some cases have ancient precedent, and, above all are inclusive.

| Inclusive | Excluding |
|---|---|
| God...God...God | God...he...he |
| God's realm | God's kingdom |
| Loving God; Mother and Father; Parent | Father |
| Ruler; Realm; Reign | King; Kingdom; Kingship |
| Child; Child of God | Son; Son of God |
| The Human One; The Representative Human | Son of Man |

This list is intended to stretch the imagination and not to limit it. Infrequently used forms in The Book of Common Prayer should be explored and utilized. The Trisagion, for example, draws attention to God as the Holy One:

> "Holy God
> Holy and Mighty
> Holy Immortal One . . ." (Holy Eucharist, Rite Two BCP p. 356)

The inclusive term "The Human One" captures the New Testament affirmation of Jesus as the archetypal or supremely representative human as well as the one from God who draws all humankind— male and female—back into the relationship with God. The inclusive terms for God protect the total otherness of God while acknowledging the divine-human relational ties, and those for Jesus encompass his maleness without suggesting that others by virtue of their sex are excluded from the redemption worked through Jesus or from sharing in that ministry.

These suggestions for making our worship more inclusive recognize that there is a problem in our religious language which increasing numbers of worshipers feel excludes, demeans, and casts persons into stereoptypic roles. The guidelines seek to go beyond this recognition by pointing to the power of language which holds for all persons the promise of redemptive self-realization in the worship of the Triune God.

# The Musical Implications of The Book of Common Prayer

## The Reverend Louis Weil

*November 1984*

Music is integral to liturgical worship. Its important role in the Christian experience of worship is often taken for granted, since it is so generally a normative aspect of corporate prayer. For the great majority of Christians, the principal service on Sunday establishes the characteristic model for liturgical worship, and that model, virtually without exception, includes musical elements. For Episcopalians, this familiar role of music as a primary element in worship is supported by the expectations indicated in the rubrics of The Book of Common Prayer.

Given the significant part which music plays in corporate worship, it is nevertheless inevitable that the musical element will vary enormously from parish to parish. Because of differences in available resources, there will be notable differences in both the character and performance of the musical aspects of liturgical celebrations. The availability of trained musicians will often permit the development of a rich tradition of choral and instrumental music in worship. Modest musical resources will imply a more modest, but no less important, role for music in the liturgy. Each congregation should aim to build a musical tradition which uses the best resources available to it.

The Book of Common Prayer demonstrates an admirable wisdom in this area, and does not, in the rubrical directions concerning music, set over-precise musical expectations. Resources vary in innumerable ways, so that musical styles which are appropriate and possible in one situation would be quite unsuitable elsewhere. For this reason, The Book of Common Prayer deals with music in a structural way. That is, the various rites clearly indicate where music of one type or another would be appropriate to the movement of a particular rite, but do not indicate stringent expectations as to what style of music will be used. This allows not only for diverse resources, but for variety of taste as well.

With regard to the musical implications of The Book of Common Prayer, it is important to learn the language of rubrics. The liturgical directions of the BCP are not chains to bind worshipers, but they are indicative of normative guidelines, and need to be interpreted with attention and sensitivity. Congregations often become accustomed to one musical pattern in liturgical worship. That pattern, however, may not correspond to the best insights available as to the role of music in corporate worship. In the BCP of 1979, there is in the rubrics a clear sense of music, not as an added-on aesthetic element, but as an integral dynamic of liturgical prayer.

In the section titled "Concerning the Service of the Church" (pp. 13–14), we find several indications related to liturgical music. One sentence is of special importance: "Where rubrics indicate that a part of a service is to be 'said,' it must be understood to include 'or sung' and *vice versa*." In other words, the BCP does not set any limit to the use of music for the various liturgical texts (other than common sense), nor does it set a requirement for musical performance upon ministers or people where those gifts are lacking. It should be noted, however, that it is with regard to the singing or non-singing of certain liturgical texts (*e.g.* the Creed, the Lord's Prayer) that congregations often develop the most fixed expectations. The BCP itself is quite flexible in this matter. In other words, a decision on this question must rest upon factors other than rubrics. For example, the poetic and hymnic texts which are integral to the various rites should be seen in their nature as *musical* elements of the ritual action. This apples to texts which are often said, even when musical resources are quite adequate to their being sung, at least in simple settings, such as the *Gloria in excelsis* and the *Sanctus*.

The reason this idea may seem strange to some Episcopalians, even many who attend parishes where music enjoys a certain prominence, is that congregational music is often conceived of narrowly in terms of hymns, and choral music in terms of an anthem at the Offertory. In other words, the poetic texts which are part of the rite itself are often said, whereas other texts, in hymns or anthems, are inserted around the primary liturgical elements.

The rubrics of the BCP allow, of course, for the appropriate incorporation of hymnody within the liturgical framework, and by and large the appointed places are those to which most Episcopalians are accustomed, as at the opening of a liturgy or at the Offertory. For important structural reasons, there is no rubrical authorization for hymns at two places where past practice created different expectations. First, no hymn is authorized at the Eucharist between the reading of the Gospel and the preaching of the sermon, in order to emphasize the underlying unity between the two, a unity which should not be violated. Secondly, in order to respect the meaning of the Dismissal, there is no authorization for a hymn at the end of Morning or Evening Prayer or at the end of the Eucharist. This purpose is supported by rubrics on p. 143 ("If an additional hymn is desired, it may be sung immediately before the Blessing or Dismissal"), and on p. 409 ("A hymn may be sung before or after the postcommunion prayer.").

More significant, however, are the implications of the rubrics of the BCP concerning the poetic texts which are integral to the rites. Within the eucharistic rite, the most obvious examples are the two referred to earlier, the *Gloria in excelsis* and the *Sanctus*. These texts are hymns of praise and adoration as much as are many metrical hymns, but with the difference that they are also part of the liturgical text. The same applies to the *Kyrie* or the *Trisagion,* and also to the *Agnus Dei*. The norm ought to be that, whenever possible, such texts should be sung rather than said. The rubrical priority for singing which appears at each occurrence of these texts supports that opinion. Among these texts, the *Sanctus* enjoys a preeminence because it is part of the eucharistic prayer and not an optional insert, as is the entrance chant of the *Agnus Dei*. There is no reason why the poetic texts mentioned in this paragraph should not be sung even at services where there is neither metrical hymnody nor choir anthems.

When we turn to a consideration of the Psalter, its use in public worship raises the same issue. The psalms are essentially poetic texts which plead for a musical setting as the preferable mode for their use in the liturgy. In spite of their nature as liturgical poetry, the custom of their being recited rather than sung has tended to prevail in the Episcopal Church. As a result, many members of the Church have often experienced the Psalter as a rather lifeless aspect of liturgical worship, in spite of the fact that particular psalms play a significant role in private prayer.

In "Concerning the Psalter," the psalm section of the BCP is introduced with these words:

> "The Psalter is a body of liturgical poetry. It is designed for vocal, congregational use, whether by singing or reading. There are several traditional methods of psalmody. The exclusive use of a single method makes the recitation of the Psalter needlessly monotonous." (BCP, p. 582)

Of the four "Traditional methods" which are there discussed, the first three are characteristically musical. Responsive recitation is acknowledged as "the method which has been most frequently used in Episcopal churches." The other three methods (direct, antiphonal and responsorial recitation) are more effectively used with music. The appeal for variety of use thus implies at least an occasional incorporation of musical settings of the psalms in corporate worship. Such variety in the use of the Psalter would serve as a corrective to the common experience of the psalms as a long block of recited material and would contribute to their rediscovery as the poetry of prayer. The diversity of the psalms should not be obscured by a monochrome pattern in liturgical use, and music offers the most obvious means to explore that diversity in the context of corporate worship.

Other obvious examples of hymnic texts are the Invitatory Psalm,

*Venite* or *Jubilate Deo,* in Morning Prayer, and the hymn *Phos hilaron* at the beginning of Evening Prayer. These texts are poetic and imply a musical rendering, and the rubrical indications confirm that a sung setting is preferred. The support of the BCP for the priority of musical versions for such poetic texts is shown in still another way: flexibility is permitted with regard to the authorized version of the text, so that "Metrical versions of the Invitatory Psalms, and of the Canticles after the Readings, may be used" (p. 141). This would permit the use of an easy or familiar hymn tune to facilitate the incorporation of a sung setting. Further, for apparently the same reason, "In place of a Canticle, a hymn may be sung" (p. 142) and, similarly, the *Gloria in excelsis* may be replaced by "some other song of praise" (p. 324, p. 256), so that, presumably, the basic meaning of the text may be proclaimed in song even if it is not possible for a musical version of the specific text to be sung.

Underlying the rubrical directions of the BCP, we find the implication that music be as integrated an element as possible in the liturgical celebration. The flexibility of the rubrics, however, implies other areas of responsible judgment for the carrying out of that implication. These areas might be defined in terms of musical, liturgical, and pastoral judgment. The music chosen must correspond realistically to the resources available. Within those limitations, what is the best and most appropriate music for a given liturgical context? This question points to the liturgical judgment concerning any music selected, that it respect the integrity of the liturgical texts and structure, so that the music remains integral to the liturgical action and does not become supplementary performance by professionals.

Musical and liturgical considerations must not be isolated from pastoral concerns. The whole liturgical act is the corporate prayer of a specific group of people who live in a particular cultural and social context. The whole of their common prayer is an expression of faith. Inappropriate music does not contribute to the nurture of that faith, but music conceived from the inner core of the liturgical act and sensitive to the pastoral reality has remarkable power for the uniting of God's people in common praise.

## BIBLIOGRAPHY

The following books and articles deal with subjects which have been discussed in this essay.

Lionel Dakers (ed.). *The Psalms.* The Royal School of Church Music, Croydon, England 1980.

*A booklet dealing with the variety of musical forms for the use of the Psalter in the liturgy.*

Lucien Deiss. *Spirit and Song of the New Liturgy.* World Library of Sacred Music, Cincinnati 1970.

*Although the author is concerned primarily with Roman Catholic liturgy, this book deals with the relation of music to the structure of the rites in principles which are useful for Episcopalians.*

Virgil C. Funk and Gabe Huck (ed.). *Pastoral Music in Practice.* Liturgy Training Publications, Chicago 1981.

*A set of essays on the role of music in the liturgy by a variety of authors.*

Joseph Gelineau. "Music and Singing in the Liturgy," in *The Study of Liturgy,* edited by C. Jones, G. Wainwright, and E. Yarnold. Oxford University Press, New York 1978, pp. 440–454.

*Gelineau has been a major influence on the restoration of music to an integral relation with the liturgy. Both this essay and book deal with questions of music and liturgical structure.*

Marion J. Hatchett. *A Manual for Clergy and Church Musicians.* The Church Hymnal Corporation, New York 1980.

*A basic guide to the role of music in The Book of Common Prayer.*

*Music in Catholic Worship.* Bishops' Committee on the Liturgy, Washington 1972.

*An excellent summary of fundamental liturgical/musical principles.*

*Liturgical Music Today.* Bishops' Committee on the Liturgy, Washington 1982.

*A statement of the R.C. Bishops' Committee on the Liturgy on the tenth anniversary of the document Music in Catholic Worship, and a very useful complement to the earlier document.*

Don E. Saliers. "The Integrity of Sung Prayer," in *Worship,* Vol. 55, No. 4, pp. 290–303.

*An essay by a Methodist who is both a fine liturgical scholar and a gifted musician.*

# Architectural Implications of The Book of Common Prayer

## The Reverend Marion J. Hatchett
*March 1985*

Different houses dictate differences in lifestyle; changes in lifestyle often dictate a move or remodeling. Through most of Church history, worship patterns have determined architectural settings. Changes in worship patterns, such as those which occurred in the fourth, the eleventh, or the sixteenth centuries, have sparked re-thinking of architectural settings. In the mid-nineteenth century, however, the medieval Gothic church came to be accepted as the ideal, and the building began to determine the worship rather than the worship determining the setting. This model fostered worship in which the members of the congregation were more or less passive spectators rather than active participants.

The Book of Common Prayer 1979 seriously challenges the suit-ability of this architectural model. It sets forth clearly a pattern which calls for Daily Morning and Evening Prayer as regular services and the Holy Eucharist as the principal service on Sundays and Holy Days. The Liturgy of the Word has its own integrity. The congregational nature of Baptism and Confirmation is stressed. All rites involve congregational participation, and many involve processions or other movements. The book provides for Reconciliation of a Penitent, for reservation of the eucharistic elements, and for use of chrism (oil of baptism) and of oil for the sick. Many provisions and new or recovered emphases of the Book of Common Prayer have architectural implications.

What follows, then, may be of real help to a congregation planning a new building or extensive remodeling within an existing building. We hope that others also will find this paper of interest and helpful.

## The Three Liturgical Centers

The rite for the Consecration of a Church makes clear that the church contains not one but three liturgical centers: the place of Baptism (font), the place of the Word (ambo, pulpit, lectern), and the place of the Eucharist (altar-table). These should stand out, and should have approximately equal dignity and prominence. They might be set off from other furnishings by use of rich or contrasting materials, vivid colors, or elaboration of decoration.

The Font—The font should be in a prominent place, so that baptisms are visible, and to be a constant reminder of baptism. It might be at the back of the nave near a principal door, in the chancel, on the floor at the front of the nave, or at the center of a large entrance hall.

Since the Book of Common Prayer gives precedence to immersion as the mode of baptism, the font might well be large enough for immersion; at the very least it should be of significant size. The font, or the area around it, might be decorated with biblical types or symbols of baptism. A convenient table or shelf should be provided for books, towels, baptismal candles, and the chrism. An aumbry (a locked case) for the chrism might be located near the font, and the Paschal Candle should normally stand at the font, except during the Great Fifty Days.

The Pulpit—The pulpit symbolizes Christ's presence in his Word as the altar symbolizes his presence in the eucharistic sacrament. Ideally, one pulpit should be used for the lessons, the gradual psalm, the Gospel, and the sermon; and also for the *Exsultet* at the Easter Vigil. It should be a prominent piece of furniture, that can accomodate a large Bible, and with a shelf for other books or items. Its construction and placement should allow torchbearers to stand near the reader. It should be accessible, so that lectors, the cantor, the reader of the Gospel, and the preacher (and possibly the leader of the Prayers of the People) can make their way to and from it easily and with dignity. The pulpit and the area around it might be decorated with symbols of the Scriptures, or of the Scriptures being read, translated, or preached.

The Altar-Table—Until the very late medieval period, when eucharistic piety centered on the elevation of the host, altars were normally rather small, typically about as wide and as deep as they were high, symbolizing an altar of sacrifice and a table of fellowship. Larger altars tend to dwarf the other liturgical centers and to create a barrier between clergy and people, rather than serving as a table around which clergy and people gather. The altar should be far enough from any wall or other furniture for movement around it to be dignified and easy. The altar and the area around it might be decorated with biblical types and symbols of the Eucharist. It is not necessary that the altar be in the center of the chancel; in fact, an off-center location may be a good solution in many cases, for the focus moves with the movement of the rite. There should only be one altar in the room.

## Other Furnishings and Ornaments

Other furnishings should be subordinate to font, pulpit, and altar.

Credence—The credence should be convenient to the altar but unobtrusive. It should be large enough to accommodate all the vessels and linens needed at the largest services, as well as the altar book and offering plates. If ablutions are done in the chancel, the credence should be large enough to serve this purpose as well.

Oblations Table—In the entrance hall or near the back of the church, there should be an oblations table large enough for the containers in which the bread and wine will be brought to the altar, for the offering plates, and possibly for food offerings and other offerings as well.

Chairs for the Liturgical Ministers—A chair for the celebrant or officiant should be in a visible position. It should be easily moveable so that it can be placed at the entrance to the chancel for confirmations and ordinations. It is sometimes best for the celebrant's chair to be on a low platform, but it must not be raised so high that it looks like a throne. Chairs or benches for assisting ministers should be grouped about the chair of the chief celebrant. The chairs should have arms and shelves (or there should be a shelf or table nearby) for books needed in the course of the service.

The Paschal Candlestand—This largest and most prominent of the candlestands is placed beside the pulpit during the Great Fifty Days. It should be tall enough to hold the candle in position to provide light for the *Exsultet* and readings of the Easter Vigil. It should be moveable, for it stands at the head of the casket at burial, and near the font outside the Great Fifty Days. It might be decorated with symbols of the Exodus, the Resurrection, and Baptism.

Other Candlesticks—The number or arrangement of candles can be varied according to the day, season, or occasion. If any candlesticks are to be placed on the altar, they should be low to focus attention on the bread and cup rather than up and away from them. Processional candlesticks with floor stands are normally preferable.

The Cross—A processional cross, designed to be placed in a floor stand near the altar, is an attractive alternative to a cross permanently hung or fixed to a wall. Normally, only one cross should be carried in procession or be visible during a rite; others may distract and weaken the symbolism.

Liturgical Books—Any book used by a liturgical minister should be "of appropriate size and dignity."

Banners, Flags, etc.—Banners, flags, hangings, etc., marking days, seasons, or occasions, may be temporary and homemade and look it; if permanent or reusable they should be the best art-work available. Symbols identified with particular cultures, groups, or nations are not appropriate as permanent parts of the liturgical environment.

60

Flowers—Flowers can highlight days or seasons and give emphasis to the three liturgical centers. The quantity, arrangement, and placement should vary with the days and occasions.

Audiovisuals—A good audio system may need to be provided, and if visual presentations are contemplated, an adequate projection system should be provided as well.

## Liturgical Space

The Chancel—There should be a low platform for the liturgical ministers. It should not, however, be so high as to seem like a stage, setting the ministers apart from the congregation. It should contain the pulpit, altar-table, and chairs for the liturgical ministers, in due relationship to each other, and so arranged that the congregation can see the person officiating, whether at a chair, the pulpit, or the altar. It should also contain a credence in an unobtrusive location. Consideration might also be given to making chancel furniture moveable.

The Nave—Requirements of a nave are somewhat different from those of an auditorium. Acoustics must be live enough to encourage vocal participation. People must be able to see and hear what goes on at the three principal liturgical centers. Seating arrangement should encourage an atmosphere of community. Adequate processional space must be provided. For a feeling of community and to foster involvement in the action in the chancel, a nave should be relatively wide in proportion to its length. The space should be unified, neither cut up by columns for having features which distract from a sense of gathering. If there is a communion rail, it should be on the nave level and easily removable.

Seating should be flexible, so that it can be adjusted for various sizes of congregations and for various rites and activities. Chairs with book racks are sometimes better than pews. It is better to provide substantial overflow space in the entrance hall than to build a nave so large that the normal congregation looks and feels lost in the space. The stations of the Way of the Cross, if used, might be represented on the floor or on the walls of the nave.

The Space for Choir and Organ—Reservation of space for the choir at the back of the congregation allows the choir to be grouped together, and the rear wall often serves as a "sounding board." For music that is properly congregational, this position is best for providing leadership and support. Moreover, when a choir anthem accompanies an action (as at the Gospel procession, the offertory, or the Communion), the congregation's attention is not so likely to be diverted from the action.

If a rear position is not possible, as in the remodeling of some buildings, the best solution is often for the choir to be placed in the old altar area facing the people and for the old choir are to become the chancel.

The choir must be in close proximity to the organ and the organist. Chairs are preferable to pews for the choir. The area should be large enough to accommodate extra singers or instrumentalists on occasion. A piano, in addition to an organ, is desirable for pre-service rehearsals and for certain types of music.

The pipes of an organ should be in the room itself, not off in an alcove, and so placed that they speak directly down its length. A qualified organ consultant should be brought into the process when a new building or a remodeling is first under consideration.

Acoustics—Proper acoustics are essential for congregational participation. Choral and instrumental music should be clear and resonant. The best acoustical conditions for hearing these several kinds of sound are frequently at variance with each other, particularly in large spaces. In any major construction or renovation, an acoustical engineer should be consulted. The effects of adding or removing any sound-absorbing materials (hangings, cushions, carpets, etc.) must be carefully considered.

Lighting—Prayer Book services demand that ministers and congregation have adequate light to read easily. Certain rites, such as the Order of Worship for the Evening and the Easter Vigil, call for flexible artificial lighting operated quietly by a person who can see and hear the liturgy. Energy efficiency, amount and movement of light admitted, and avoidance of outside distractions should govern the placement of windows and choice of materials used for them. Stained glass, though often beautiful, is not necessary, nor with some styles of architecture, even appropriate.

Processional Space—The rubrics of the Eucharist require three processions: the entrance of the liturgical ministers, the bringing of the offerings to the deacon or celebrant, and the Communion procession of the people. In addition, there may be a procession of the reader of the Gospel to the pulpit, and the movement of lectors and cantor to the pulpit and of the leader of the Prayers of the People to an appropriate place. Other rites require additional processions or movements. A center aisle seven feet wide is desirable; other aisles probably five.

There should be enough space between the chancel steps and the first row of seating for easy movement at Communion or to allow for a large group of people to gather at the front of the church (a wedding party, confirmation candidates, etc.), or to approach the altar easily when a coffin is present. The space should be large enough to allow persons in wheelchairs and on crutches to move easily.

The Entrance and Entrance Hall—The entrance should be inviting rather than formidable. At least one entrance should be accessible (barrier free) to the aged and disabled.

The entrance hall should be a generous, pleasant space for gathering and lingering. It should contain provisions for overcoats and rain gear. It should be large enough for the formation of the Palm Sunday procession, the lighting of the new fire at the Easter Vigil, the formation of wedding processions, and the reception of the body at a burial; as well as for the normal entrance processions.

## Auxiliary Spaces

Every church needs a sacristy and appropriate place for the reservation of sacramental elements and for the reconciliation of a penitent.

The Sacristy—A sacristy is a necessity. Two adjacent but separate sacristies are desirable: a working sacristy for the altar guild and a vesting sacristy for the liturgical ministers.

The vesting sacristy should contain sufficient closet and drawer space for all the vestments. There should be surface space for the laying out of vestments and the service register, and shelf space for the various liturgical books. It should contain a floor-length mirror and a prominent and dependable clock. A rest room should open off this sacristy. In this sacristy or near it should be stands or holders for processional crosses, candlesticks, banners, and thurible.

The altar guild sacristy should contain storage space for items used occasionally or seasonally (hangings, vases, Advent wreath, Christmas creche, footwashing basin, burial pall, etc.) as well as for the vessels and linens used regularly. There should be sufficient counter space for setting out eucharistic vessels and for arranging flowers. This sacristy should also contain a sink (with hot water always available), a second sink (piscina) which drains directly to the ground, cool storage for candles and wine, a small freezer for extra bread at the Eucharist, a neat bulletin board, and a bookshelf for a small collection of pertinent books. A small washing machine and dryer, and an iron and ironing board, are also desirable.

Ideally, the sacristy should provide easy access to the chancel and to the entrance hall.

The Place of Reservation—Since the Prayer Book implies that Communion of those unable to attend a public celebration is normally to be from the reserved Sacrament, and since it provides for Good Friday Communion from the elements consecrated at the Maundy Thursday celebration, and allows administration by a deacon, a church building should have a place for the reservation of the eucharistic elements. An aumbry might be fixed in the wall of the sacristy, or of a chapel, or on a side wall of the chancel out of the normal line of vision of the congregation. Preferably, the eucharistic sacrament is not reserved at an altar at which the Eucharist is celebrated.

The Prayer Book provides for use of two oils: baptismal chrism and the oil for the sick. The oil of chrism might be reserved in an aumbry near the font, or both oils might be reserved in an aumbry in the sacristy. This aumbry should be large enough to hold several sealed cruets containing sufficient chrism for the several baptism days, and oil for the anointing of the sick.

The Place for the Reconciliation of a Penitent—The Prayer Book suggests that this rite might take place in the church building with the penitent kneeling and the confessor seated, or that the confessor and penitent might sit face to face; or, if thought desirable, a room near the baptismal area, furnished simply and austerely, with provisions for confession in either posture, might be provided.

## Procedure When Contemplating Building or Remodeling

The first step in any building or remodeling program is a many-faceted educational one. The congregation needs to be brought to an appreciation of the spirit and rationale of the rites of the Book of Common Prayer and the Book of Occasional Services and their architectural implications. It needs to consider broader needs of the community (especially needs of the poor, the handicapped and the oppressed) and the possibility of sharing facilities with other organizations. Formation of a building committee should come out of such a soul-searching educational process. At an early stage, an organ consultant and consultants in liturgy, art, and acoustics should be brought into the planning. The building committee then needs to begin work with an architect.

Responsible stewardship of the people's offerings and of natural resources dictates that any new building or remodeling be done with consideration for efficient use of energy, including investigation of passive and active solar heating. Consideration should be given to multiple uses of spaces (including entrance hall and nave), and to how minimal space might be fully heated or cooled through the week.

Responsible stewardship also dictates that unnecessary restraints not be placed on future uses of the facilities. For example, there should be a few load-bearing walls in an office area or area set apart for Christian education so that these areas can more easily and more economically be rearranged as methods and staff change. Some furnishings, such as organ and font, may have to be fixed, but maximum flexibility is desirable.

Throughout the process, the architect and building committee must be conscious of accessibility (barrier free) to the aged and disabled and keep alert to find additional ways in which the building might be made more useful for serving the needs of the community surrounding it.

## BIBLIOGRAPHY

Addleshaw, G.W.O. and Etchells, F. *The Architectural Setting of Anglican Worship.* London: Faber and Faber, 1948.

Bishops' Commitee on the Liturgy. *Environment and Art in Catholic Worship.* Washington: United States Catholic Conference, 1978

Bruggink, D.J., and C.H. Droppers. *Christ and Architecture.* Grand Rapids: Eerdmans, 1965.

Clarke, B. and Betjeman, J. *English Churches.* London: Vista Books, 1964.

Davies, J.G. *The Architectural Setting of Baptism.* London: Barrie and Rockliff, 1962.

Davies, J.G. *The Origin and Development of Early Christian Church Architecture.* London: S.C.M. Press, 1952.

Davies, J.G. *The Secular Use of Church Buildings.* 2d ed.; New York: Pueblo.

*Faith and Form.*

Krautheimer, R. *Early Christian and Byzantine Architecture.* Harmondsworth, Middlesex: Penguin Books, 1965.

*Planning: Space for Worship.* 2d ed.; New York: Board of Global Ministries, United Methodist Church, 1976.

Sovik, E.A. *Architecture for Worship.* Minneapolis: Augsburg Publishing House, 1973.

Stanton, P.B. *The Gothic Revival and American Church Architecture: An Episode in Taste, 1840–1856.* Baltimore: Johns Hopkins Press, 1968.

Van Loon, Ralph R. *Space for Worship: Some Thoughts on Liturgy, Architecture, Art.* Philadelphia: Lutheran Church in America, 1982.

White, J.F. *The Cambridge Movement: The Ecclesiologists and the Gothic Revival.* Cambridge: University Press, 1962.

White, J.F. *Protestant Worship and Church Architecture.* New York: Oxford University Press, 1964.

# The Proposed Lesser Feasts and Fasts As Approved for Trial Use 1985–1988

*January, 1987*

Aelred was born in 1109, of a family which had long been treasurers of the shrine of Cuthbert of Lindisfarne at Durham Cathedral. While still a youth, he was sent for education in upper-class life to the court of King David of Scotland, son of Queen Margaret. The King's stepsons Simon and Waldef were his models and intimate friends. After intense disillusion and inner struggle, Aelred went to Yorkshire, where he became a Cistercian monk at the abbey of Rievaulx in 1133.

Aelred soon became a major figure in English church life. Sent to Rome on diocesan affairs by Archbishop William of York, he returned by way of Clairvaux. Here he made a deep impression on Bernard, who encouraged the young monk to write his first work, *Mirror of Charity*, on Christian perfection. In 1143, Aelred led the founding of a new Cistercian house at Revesby. Four years later he was appointed abbot of Rievaulx. By the time of his death from a painful kidney disease in 1167, the abbey had over 600 monks, including Aelred's biographer and friend, Walter Daniel. During this period, Aelred wrote his best known work, *Spiritual Friendship*.

Friendship, Aelred teaches, is both a gift from God and a creation of human effort. While love is universal, freely given to all, friendship is a particular love between individuals, of which the example is Jesus and John the Beloved Disciple. As abbot, Aelred allowed his monks to hold hands and give other expressions of friendship. In the spirit of Anselm of Canterbury and Bernard of Clairvaux, Aelred writes:

> There are four qualities which characterize a friend: loyalty, right intention, discretion, and patience. Right intention seeks for nothing other than God and natural good. Discretion brings understanding of what is done on a friend's behalf, and ability to know when to correct faults. Patience enables one to be justly rebuked, or to bear adversity on another's behalf. Loyalty guards and protects friendship, in good or bitter times.

# Aelred

*Abbott of Rievaulx, 1167*

I    Pour thou into our hears, we beseech thee, O God, the Holy Spirit's gift of love, that we, clasping each the other's hand, may share the joy of friendship, human and divine, and with thy servant Aelred draw many into thy community of love; through Jesus Christ the Righteous, who liveth and reigneth with thee in the unity of the Holy Spirit, one God, now and forever. *Amen.*

II    Pour into our hearts, O God, the Holy Spirit's gift of love, that we, clasping each the other's hand, may share the joy of friendship, human and divine, and with your servant Aelred draw many to your community of love; through Jesus Christ the Righteous, who lives and reigns with you, in the unity of the Holy Spirit, one God, now and forever. *Amen.*

| Psalm | Lessons |
|-------|---------|
| 36:5–10 | Philippians 2:1–4 |
| *or* 145:8–13 | John 15:9–17 |
| | *or* Mark 12:28–34a |

*Preface of a Saint (2)*

The life of Martin Luther King, Jr., exemplified his profound conviction that all persons, regardless of race, nationality, or religion, are interdependent in an inescapable network of mutuality. He dedicated his life to the creation of "the beloved community" of love, justice, and peace.

King was born on January 15, 1929, in Atlanta, Georgia. As the son and grandson of Baptist preachers, he was steeped in the Black Church tradition. To this heritage he added a thorough academic preparation, earning the degrees of Bachelor of Arts, Bachelor of Divinity, and a Doctor of Philosophy in Systematic Theology from Boston University. In Boston he met and married Coretta Scott, by whom he had four children.

King accepted a call in 1954 to become pastor of a church in Montgomery, Alabama. There, Black indignation at inhumane treatment on segregated buses culminated in December, 1955, in the arrest of Rosa Parks for refusing to give up her seat to a white man. King was catapulted into national prominence as the leader of the Montgomery bus boycott. He became increasingly the articulate prophet, who could not only rally the Black masses, but could also move the consciences of Whites.

King founded the Southern Christian Leadership Conference to spearhead non-violent mass demonstrations against racism. Many confrontations followed, most notably in Birmingham and Selma, Alabama, and in Chicago.

On August 28, 1963, King electrified nearly 250,000 persons, who had marched to Washington for "Jobs and Freedom," by his "I have a dream" speech at the Lincoln Memorial.

King's campaigns were instrumental to the passage of the Civil Rights acts of 1964, 1965 and 1968. With the dismantling of segregation and disenfranchisement, he turned his attention to economic empowerment of the poor and opposition to the Vietnam War, contending that racism, poverty and militarism were interrelated.

King lived in constant danger; his home was dynamited, he was almost fatally stabbed, and was harassed by death threats. He was jailed some 30 times, and the FBI sought to discredit him, suspecting him of having communist connections. Through it all, he was sustained by his deep faith.

In 1957, after an exhausting day, he received, late at night, a vicious telephone threat. Alone in his kitchen, he wept and prayed. He relates that he heard the Lord speaking to him and saying, "Martin Luther, stand up for righteousness, stand up for justice.", and promising never to leave him alone —"No, never alone." King refers to this vision as his "Mountain-top Experience."

After preaching at Washington Cathedral on Passion Sunday, March 31, 1968, King went to Memphis, Tennessee, in support of sanitation workers in their struggle for better wages. There, he proclaimed that he had been "to the mountain-top" and had seen "the Promised Land," and that he knew that one day he and his people would be "free at last." On the following day, April 4, he was cut down by an assassin's bullet.

# Martin Luther King, Jr.

*Civil Rights Leader, 1968*

I  Almighty God, who by the hand of Moses thy servant didst lead thy people out of slavery, and didst make them free at last: Grant that thy Church, following the example of thy prophet Martin Luther King, may resist oppression in the name of thy love, and may strive to secure for all thy children the blessed liberty of the Gospel of Jesus Christ; who liveth and reigneth with thee and the Holy Spirit, one God, now and forever. *Amen.*

II  Almighty God, by the hand of Moses your servant you led your people out of slavery, and made them free at last: Grant that your Church, following the example of your prophet Martin Luther King, may resist oppression in the name of your love, and may secure for all your children the blessed liberty of the Gospel of Jesus Christ; who lives and reigns with you and the Holy Spirit, one God, now and for ever. *Amen.*

| Psalm | Lessons |
|---|---|
| 77:11–20 | Exodus 3:7–12 |
| | Luke 6:27–36 |

*Preface of the Epiphany*

"God's warrior" is an epithet by which David Pendleton Oakerhater is known among the Cheyenne Indians of Oklahoma. The title is an apt one, for this apostle of Christ to the Cheyenne was originally a soldier who fought against the United States government with warriors of other tribes in the disputes over Indian land rights. By the late 1860s Oakerhater had distinguished himself for bravery and leadership as an officer in an elite corps of Cheyenne fighters. In 1875, after a year of minor uprisings and threats of major violence, he and twenty-seven other warrior leaders were taken prisoner by the U.S. Army, charged with inciting rebellion, and sent to a disused military prison compound in Florida.

Under the influence of a concerned Army captain, who sought to educate the prisoners, Oakerhater and his companions learned English, gave art and archery lessons to the area's many visitors, and had their first encounter with the Christian faith. The captain's example, and that of other concerned Christians, from as far away as New York, had their effect on the young warrior. He was moved to answer the call to transform his leadership in war into a lifelong ministry of peace.

With sponsorship from the Diocese of Central New York and financial help from a Mrs. Pendleton of Cincinnati, he and three other prisoners went north to study for the ministry. At his baptism in Syracuse in 1878 he took the name David Pendleton Oakerhater, in honor of his benefactress.

Soon after his ordination to the diaconate in 1881, David returned to Oklahoma. There, he was instrumental in founding and operating schools and missions, through great personal sacrifice and often in the face of apathy from the Church hierarchy and resistance from the government. He continued his ministry of service, education, and pastoral care among his people until his death on August 31, 1931.

Half a century before, the young deacon had told his people: "You all know me. You remember when I led you out to war I went first, and what I told you was true. Now I have been away to the East and I haved learned about another captain, the Lord Jesus Christ, and he is my leader. He goes first, and all he tells me is true. I come back to my people to tell you to go with me now in this new road, a war that makes all for peace."

# David Pendleton Oakerhater

*Deacon and Missionary of the Cheyenne, 1931*

I   O God of unsearchable wisdom and infinite mercy, thou didst choose a captive warrior, David Oakerhater, to be thy servant, and didst send him to be a missionary to his own people and to execute the office of a deacon among them: Liberate us, who commemorate him today, from bondage of self, and empower us for service to thee and to the neighbors thou hast given us; through Jesus Christ, the captain of our salvation; who liveth and reigneth with thee and the Holy Spirit, one God for ever and ever. *Amen.*

II   O God of unsearchable wisdom and infinite mercy, you chose a captive warrior, David Oakerhater, to be your servant, and sent him to be a missionary to his own people, and to exercise the office of a deacon among them: Liberate us, who commemorate him today, from bondage to self, and empower us for service to you and to the neighbors you have given us; through Jesus Christ, the captain of our salvation; who lives and reigns with you and the Holy Spirit, one God, for ever and ever. *Amen.*

| Psalm | Lessons |
|---|---|
| 96:1–7 | Isaiah 52:7–10 |
| *or* 98:1–4 | Luke 10:1–9 |

*Preface of Apostles*

When four Sisters of the Community of St. Mary came to Memphis in 1873, at the invitation of Bishop Quintard, to begin a school for girls, and to establish a Church home for the ill and needy, they were confronted almost immediately with an epidemic of yellow fever. Instead of opening a school, the Sisters cared for the sick in the Cathedral District. Once that epidemic ended, with the coming of cool weather, Sisters Constance, Thecla, and Hughetta opened the school. The fourth Sister, Amelia, administered the new Church home.

In 1878, the plague struck again, with a virulence far exceeding that of 1873. City-dwellers who could fled the city in great numbers, including doctors and many of the clergy. The Episcopal and Roman Catholic clerics and nuns, several Methodist clerics, a few doctors (including the Sisters' physician, Dr. Armstrong), remained. To aid, Sisters Ruth and Helen came from the Order's Motherhouse, along with Sister Clare, a nurse, from the Society of St. Margaret. Sister Constance, in effect the Prioress, has left records of the fearful inroads of the epidemic. She found the sick and dying, and the dead, abandoned by the healthy; she found persons spurned by their own relatives and friends.

A local cleric, the Reverend Mr. Parsons, wrote, "the Sisters are doing wonderful work. . .These brave, unshrinking daughters of the Divine Love can accomplish so much in efforts and results.", this in a letter to Bishop Quintard. Soon after, the Reverend Mr. Parsons died. The Reverend D.T. Dalzell from Shreveport, a priest and a medical doctor, volunteered his services, as did the Reverend Louis Schuyler from New Jersey.

Within a little over two weeks, Sister Constance died (on September 9), followed closely by Dr. Armstrong, Sister Thecla, the Reverend Mr. Schuyler, Sister Ruth, Mrs. Bullock (a devoted laywoman), and Sister Frances. At least twelve Roman Catholic clerics and thirty-four Roman Catholic nuns died, as did a Methodist minister. The Sisters who remained, Clare, Helen, and Hughetta, continued their ministry against overwhelming odds.

Finally, cold, dry weather came and abated the epidemic conditions.

Knowledge of the courageous work of the Roman Catholic and Episcopal clerics and lay persons was spread widely through the nation's newspapers. One account spoke of the Sisters of St. Mary, and other religious, saying, "They won for their Orders an imperishable renown. They proved that Christian heroism and Christ-like self-denial are not the virtues of a particular sect." The Reverend James De Koven, a noted Churchman from Wisconsin, saw the deaths of the Sisters as "giving the Sisterhood a place in the hearts of people which cannot be shaken."

The four Sisters, sharing burial plots with some of the Roman Catholic clerics and nuns and the Methodist minister, with Dr. Armstrong, the Reverend Mr. Parson, and Mrs. Bullock—these are "The Martyrs of Memphis," witnesses to the loving work of the great Physician, through his beloved and loving children.

# Constance, Nun, and her Companions

*Commonly called "The Martyrs of Memphis," 1878*

I   We give thee thanks and praise, O God of compassion, for the heroic witness of Constance and her companions, who, in a time of plague and pestilence, were steadfast in their care for the sick and dying, and loved not their own lives, even unto death: Inspire in us a like love and commitment to those in need, following the example of our Savior Jesus Christ; who with thee and the Holy spirit liveth and reigneth, one God, now and for ever. *Amen.*

II   We give you thanks and praise, O God of compassion, for the heroic witness of Constance and her companions, who, in a time of plague and pestilence, were steadfast in their care for the sick and dying, and loved not their own lives, even unto death: Inspire in us a like love and commitment to those in need, following the example of our Savior Jesus Christ; who with you and the Holy Spirit lives and reigns, one God, now and for ever. *Amen.*

| Psalm | Lessons |
|---|---|
| 116:1–8 | 2 Corinthians 1:3–5 |
| or 116:10–17 | John 12:24–28 |

*Preface of a Saint (1)*

Teresa was one of two women declared a "Doctor of the Church" in 1970, primarily because of her two mystical contemplative works, *The Way of Perfection* and *Interior Castle.* She was a close spiritual and personal friend of St. John of the Cross, to whom she looked as a mentor and participant in the mystic experience.

Teresa was born into a family of substance near Avila. Even in her childhood, she took much pleasure in the study of saints' lives, and she used to delight in spending times of contemplation, repeating over and over "For ever, for ever, for ever, for ever, they shall see God."

In her autobiography Teresa tells that, following her mother's death, she became quite worldly. To offset this, her father placed her in an Augustinian convent to be educated with other young women of rank, but serious illness ended her studies. During convalescence, she determined to enter the religious life; and, though opposed by her father, she became a postulant at a Carmelite convent. Again, illness forced her to return home. Finally recovering good health after three years, she returned to the convent.

The easygoing life of the "mitigated" Carmelite rule—visitors from outside were freely admitted to converse with the religious, sisters could own property and have the comforts of the secular world, free from its responsibilities —distracted her from her customary prayer life, to which she returned. Taking recourse in two great penitents, Augustine of Hippo and Mary Magdalene, she became increasingly meditative. She began to receive visions— whether from God or the Devil she and her confidants could not know— and struggled to reject them. One day, while reciting the *Veni Creator Spiritus,* she was seized with rapture and heard "I will not have you hold conversation with men but with angels. . ."

Teresa set out with determination to establish a reformed Carmelite order of the "discalced" religious, who wore sandals or went unshod. Despite many setbacks, frustrations, disappointments, and lack of financial resources, she traveled for 25 years through Spain, often indigent, without food or decent lodging. Energetic, practical, efficient, as well as being a mystic and ascetic, she established 17 convents of Reformed Carmelites. Even imprisonment did not deter her or her companion mystic, St. John, who administered the two orders for men.

Despite the demands of her administrative and missionary work, Teresa found time to write the numerous letters that give us rare insights into her personality and concerns. She shows us a practical organizer, a writer of native genius, a warm devoted friend, and, above all, a lover of and the beloved of God.

Her death, following two years of illness that did not deter her from "doing with all her might," was peaceful. Her last sight was of the Sacrament brought for her comfort; her last words, "O my Lord!, now is the time that we may see each other."

# Teresa of Avila, Nun
*1582*

I    O God, who by thy Holy Spirit didst move Teresa of Avila to manifest to thy Church the way of perfection: Grant us, we beseech thee, to be nourished by her excellent teaching, and enkindle within us a lively and unquenchable longing for true holiness; through Jesus Christ, the joy of loving hearts, who with thee and the same Holy Spirit liveth and reigneth, one God, for ever and ever. *Amen.*

II    O God, by your Holy Spirit you moved Teresa of Avila to manifest to your Church the way of perfection: Grant us, we pray, to be nourished by her excellent teaching, and enkindle within us a keen and unquenchable longing for true holiness; through Jesus Christ, the joy of loving hearts, who with you and the Holy Spirit lives and reigns, one God, for ever and ever. *Amen.*

| Psalm | Lessons |
|-------|---------|
| 42:1–7 | Romans 8:22–27 |
| *or* 139:1–9 | Matthew 5:13–16 |

*Preface of Baptism*

Edmund ascended the throne of East Anglia at the age of fifteen, one of several monarchs who ruled various parts of England at that period in her history. The principle source of information about the martyrdom of the young king is an account by Dunstan, who became Archbishop of Canterbury ninety years after Edmund's death. Dunstan had heard the story many years before from a man who claimed to have been Edmund's armor bearer.

Edmund had reigned as a Christian king for nearly fifteen years when Danish armies invaded England in 870. Led by two brothers, Hinguar and Hubba, the Danes moved south, burning monasteries and churches, plundering and destroying entire villages, and killing hundreds. Upon reaching East Anglia, the brothers confronted Edmund and offered to share their treasure with him if he would acknowledge their supremacy, forbid all practice of the Christian faith, and become a figurehead ruler. Edmund's bishops advised him to accept the terms and avoid further bloodshed, but the king refused. He declared that he would not forsake Christ by surrendering to pagan rule, nor would he betray his people by consorting with the enemy.

Edmund's small army fought bravely against the Danes, but the king was eventually captured. According to Dunstan's account, Edmund was tortured, beaten, shot through with arrows, and finally beheaded. By tradition, the date of his death is November 20, 870.

The cult of the twenty-nine-year-old martyr grew very rapidly, and his remains were eventually enshrined in a Benedictine monastery in Bedericesworth—now called Bury St. Edmunds. Through the centuries Edmund's shrine became a traditional place of pilgrimage for England's kings, who came to pray at the grave of a man who remained steadfast in the Christian faith and loyal to the integrity of the English people.

# Edmund

*King of East Anglia, Martyr, 870*

I    O God of ineffable mercy, thou didst give grace and fortitude to blessed Edmund the king to triumph over the enemy of his people by nobly dying for thy Name: Bestow on us thy servants, we beseech thee, the shield of faith, wherewith we may withstand the assaults of our ancient enemy; through Jesus Christ our Redeemer, who liveth and reigneth with thee and the Holy Spirit, one God, now and for ever. *Amen.*

II    O God of ineffable mercy, you gave grace and fortitude to blessed Edmund the king to triumph over the enemy of his people by nobly dying for your Name: Bestow on us your servants the shield of faith with which we can withstand the assaults of our ancient enemy; through Jesus Christ our Redeemer, who lives and reigns with you and the Holy Spirit, one God, now and for ever. *Amen.*

| Psalm | Lessons |
|-------|---------|
| 21:1–7 | 1 Peter 3:14–18 |
| *or* 126 | Matthew 10:16–22 |

*Preface of Baptism*

In the Rule for the Order of the Holy Cross, James Huntington wrote: "Holiness is the brightness of divine love, and love is never idle; it must accomplish great things." This commitment to active ministry firmly rooted in the spiritual life was the guiding principle for the founder of the first permanent Episcopal monastic community for men in the United States.

James Otis Sargent Huntington was born in Boston in 1854. After his graduation from Harvard in 1875, he studied theology at St. Andrew's Divinity School in Syracuse, New York, and was ordained deacon and priest by his father, the first Bishop of Central New York. In 1880 and 1881 he ministered in a working-class congregation at Calvary Mission in Syracuse.

While attending a retreat at St. Clement's Church in Philadelphia, a leading parish in the Catholic revival, Huntington received a call to the religious life. He considered joining the Society of St. John the Evangelist, which had by that time established a province in the United States, but he resolved to found an indigenous American community which would reflect the sensibilities of the American Church.

Huntington and two other priests began their common life at Holy Cross Mission on New York's Lower East Side, ministering with the Sisters of St. John Baptist among poor European immigrants. The taxing daily regimen of Eucharist, prayer, and long hours of pastoral work soon forced one priest to leave for reason of health. The other dropped out for lack of a monastic vocation. Huntington went on alone; and on November 25, 1884, his life vow was received by Bishop Henry Codman Potter of New York.

As Huntington continued his work among the immigrants, with a special emphasis on helping young people, he became increasingly committed to the social witness of the Church. His early involvements in the single-tax movement and the labor union movement were instrumental in the eventual programmatic commitment of the Episcopal Church to social ministries.

The Order attracted vocations, and as it grew in the ensuing years the community moved, first to Maryland, and, in 1902, to West Park, New York, where it established the monastery which is its mother house. Huntington served as Superior on several occasions, continuing his energetic round of preaching, teaching and spiritual counsel until his death on June 28, 1935.

# James Otis Sargent Huntington

*Priest and Monk, 1935*

I  O loving God, by thy grace thy servant James Huntington gathered a community dedicated to love and discipline and devotion to the holy Cross of our Savior Jesus Christ: Send thy blessing upon all who proclaim Christ crucified, and move the hearts of many to look unto him and be saved; who with thee and the Holy Spirit liveth and reigneth, one God, for ever and ever. *Amen.*

II  O loving God, by your grace your servant James Huntington gathered a community dedicated to love and discipline and devotion to the holy Cross of our Savior Jesus Christ: Send your blessing on all who proclaim Christ crucified, and move the hearts of many to look upon him and be saved; who with you and the Holy spirit lives and reigns, one God, for ever and ever. *Amen.*

| Psalm | Lessons |
|---|---|
| 119:161–168 | Galatians 6:14–18 |
| *or* 34:1–8 | John 4:34–38 |

*Preface of a Saint (2)*

Within a year of ascending the throne in 1855, the twenty year old King Kamehameha IV and his bride, Emma Rooke, embarked on the path of altruism and unassuming humility for which they have been revered by their people. The year before, Honolulu, and especially its native Hawaiians, had been horribly afflicted by smallpox. Thousands died. The people, accustomed to a royalty which ruled with pomp and power, were confronted instead by a king and queen who went about from household to household, "with notebook in hand," soliciting from rich and poor the funds to build a hospital for the suffering populace. Queen's Hospital, named for Queen Emma, is now the largest civilian hospital in Hawaii.

In 1860, the king and queen petitioned Wilberforce, Bishop of Oxford, to send missionaries to establish the Anglican Church in Hawaii. The king's interest came through a boyhood tour of England where he had seen, in the stately beauty of Anglican liturgy, a quality that seemed more attuned to the gentle beauty of the Hawaiian spirit than the rather stark and rigorous Congregationalism imported with the whalers and merchants of New England. England responded by sending the Rt. Rev. Thomas N. Staley and two priests. They arrived on October 11, 1862, and the King and Queen were confirmed a month later, on November 28, 1862. They then began preparations for a cathedral and school, and the king set about to translate The Book of Common Prayer and much of the Hymnal for his people.

King Kamehameha IV's life was marred by the tragic death of his four year old son and only child, in 1863. The king seemed unable to survive his sadness, although a sermon he preached after his son's death expresses a hope and faith that is extraordinarily eloquent and theologically profound. His own death took place only a year after his son's, in 1864, and after only nine years as King. Emma declined to rule; instead, she committed her life to good works on behalf of her people. She was responsible for schools, churches, and countless efforts on behalf of the poor and sick. She traveled several times to England and the Continent to raise funds, and became a great favorite of Queen Victoria's. Charles Thomas Longley, Archbishop of Canterbury, remarked upon her visit to Lambeth: "I was much struck by the cultivation of her mind, and I must state that she was better informed in English literature and history than most English ladies I meet. But what excited my interest most was her deep-rooted piety, her almost saintly piety."

The cathedral the King and Queen had promised was completed in Honolulu a few months after Emma died in 1885. In one chapel stands the marble font sent by Lady Jane Franklin, intended for the baptism of the royal son, that arrived only weeks after his death. The Cathedral was named St. Andrew's in memory of the King, who died on that Saint's day in 1864. Among the Hawaiian people, Emma is still referred to, as though she had just departed, as "our beloved Queen." Though she and the King were not allowed to see much of their work completed, there has been no end to what was begun.

# Kamehameha and Emma

*King and Queen of Hawaii, 1863, 1885*

I   O sovereign God, thou didst raise up Kamehameha and Emma to be godly monarchs given to deeds of benevolence for their people and thy Church: Receive our prayers of thanksgiving for their lives and works of mercy, and by thy grace grant that we, with them and all thy faithful servants, may attain to that crown that fadeth not away; through Jesus Christ, our only Mediator and Advocate, who with thee and the Holy Spirit liveth and reigneth, one God, now and for ever. *Amen.*

II   O sovereign God, you raised up Kamehameha and Emma to be godly monarchs given to deeds of benevolence for their people and your Church: Receive our prayers of thanksgiving for their lives and works of mercy, and by your grace grant that we, with them and all your faithful servants, may attain to that crown that never fades away; through Jesus Christ, our only Mediator and Advocate, who lives and reigns with you and the Holy Spirit, one God, now and for ever. *Amen.*

| Psalm | Lessons |
|---|---|
| 33:12–22 | Acts 17:22–31 |
| *or* 97:1–2, 7–12 | Matthew 25:31–40 |

*Preface of Baptism*